Fitting Out Your Boat

in Fibreglass or Wood

Michael Naujok

ADLARD COLES NAUTICAL
London

Published 2004 by Adlard Coles Nautical
an imprint of A & C Black Publishers Ltd
37 Soho Square, London W1D 3QZ
www.adlardcoles.com

Copyright © Delius Klasing & Co KG, Bielefeld

ISBN 0-7136-6806-7

This edition published 2004

Typeset inTrump Mediaeval 9.7pt on 12.2 pt
Printed and bound in Germany

Note: While all reasonable care has been taken in the publication of this book, the publisher takes no responsibility for the use of the methods or products described in the book.

Fitting Out
Your Boat

Contents

Preface

'The road is the goal', so said the wise Confucius (551 to 479 BC). In other words, it's not just the end result but also the journey that should be fulfilling, enjoyable, and provide us with a sense of contentment.

Anything we create with our own hands, or using our own imagination, will reward us with a profound feeling of satisfaction and pride. That's why a refit which we undertake ourselves should be far more than simply an economic necessity. A refit which gives a new lease of life to something old and valuable should be a pleasure. There's also the additional bonus that in so doing, one may even improve on the original at the same time. Conversely, anyone who sees a DIY refit simply as a way of saving money on repairs won't have a lot of fun along the way.

Apart from making structural improvements, of course, one of the main aims of a refit is to enhance your boat's appearance. Many boats suffer from neglect in this area and end up as little more than merely another form of transport. True boat lovers, however, take enormous delight in a beautifully presented yacht, which again, is one of the main reasons why they enjoy keeping their own pride and joys up to scratch.

On the following pages I shall be trying to encourage you to undertake your own refit, on your own boat – a mini adventure in itself – by providing a step-by-step guide to help you reach your goal.

Special thanks are due to my son Holger and his partner Britta Herbers, who showed what might be involved by refitting their own two boats, one built in fibreglass, the other in wood. With their help I hope to make DIY refits more popular because, in my view, the time has come: thousands of old and neglected, but still structurally sound boats are waiting to be reborn! There's an enormous number of opportunities, with lots of cheap craft around at the moment. So what are we waiting for?

Michael Naujok

Do your own refit – the inexpensive way to own a proper yacht

1 This is really hard work. Removing all the old layers of paint requires strength and stamina.

There are dozens of reasons why more and more people are undertaking their own refits. For one thing, prices of new boats are rising dramatically and potential owners are finding it increasingly difficult to keep up. On the other hand, thousands of older fibreglass or plywood yachts are being laid up around our coasts. Many of them, while showing signs of obvious neglect, more often than not are still basically sound. Such boats provide the opportunity for enthusiasts to acquire low cost crafts; what's more, they can be found all over Europe – and beyond.

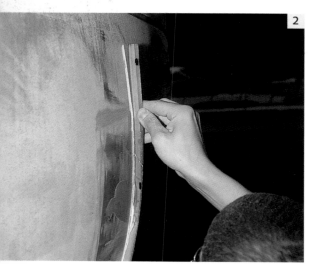

2 Scratches, cracks and other areas of damage are best filled and faired with epoxy.

Boats like this, between, say, 22 and 28 feet can be found for as little as £3500 to £7000 ($5900 to $11,800). A do-it-yourself refit might cost you another £3500 ($5900) or so, but taken together, this still represents a substantial saving on the price of a new boat. A comparable sized new boat might set you back at least £17,500 ($29,500) and possibly as much as £28,000 ($47,300) Euros.

With larger yachts, the savings you can make are even higher. Popular classics like the Nicholson 32 or the Sparkman & Stevens 35 for example command high prices on the second hand market, assuming they've been properly restored. So, carrying out a thorough refit can also be an economic way of owning a valuable asset. Having said that, it's probably fair to say that not many people will do up an old boat simply to make money.

On the other hand it's not really that difficult. It's not true that professional crafts-men are the only people who can carry out such work; all it takes is an understanding of basic do-it-yourself techniques. And that's especially true with smaller boats. The kind of work that's needed here requires no more than average skills, and makes use of fibreglass and wood working techniques which are well within the capabilities of the enthusiastic amateur. And if some of the work requires a specialist understanding – of engines, or elect-rical systems or rigging – you can always ask for expert advice. But after a refit like this, any owner will have learned a great deal. By doing the work yourself, you build up an intimate knowledge of your own boat.

In the meantime, some establishments already offer special refit facilities, where ambitious amateurs can work, using the professional infrastructure supplied by the yard. The benefits are obvious. Not only will the workplace be as good as you can possibly get it, complete with electricity, lighting and heating, but if you run into problems, professional help is at hand.

However, if you can't find a yard like that in your area, a shed will do just as well – though the closer it is to your home, the better. Often, it's merely a matter of doing small or relatively simple jobs – like fitting deck hardware, painting or varnishing small areas, or checking to see if certain parts fit. If the journey to your boat takes longer than it does to complete simple tasks like these, the situation is far from ideal.

The site for your refit must be covered and have electricity. It might be possible to do some of the preparatory jobs under a tent or an awning, but not the entire refit. To save money, some people tackle refits in two stages. The preparation work, like sanding down, filling and fairing and removing fittings can be done under an awning – while

3 Fine sanding. Bit by bit, and little by little, the hull will slowly get back into shape.

4 On with the first coat. A good primer is essential for the overall success of the paint-job.

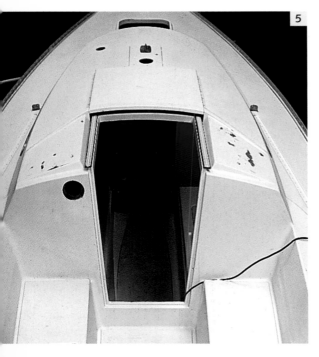

5

5 A nice empty deck. All the fittings have been completely removed so a proper job can be done.

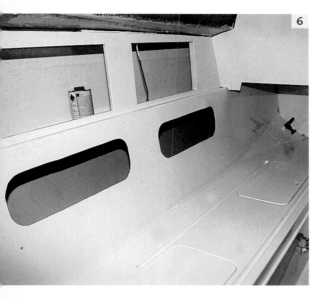

6

6 The bare interior below. As you can see, the saloon too has also been completely stripped.

the final painting, varnishing and finishing can be completed in late spring, as soon as most winter storage sheds are empty and thus cheaper to rent.

You don't really need any specialist equipment apart from a well organised toolbox and some good quality DIY power tools. Among the latter should be an electric drill with variable speeds, a battery driven screwdriver with a fast charging unit, an adjustable jigsaw, a sanding machine and an industrial type vacuum cleaner. Good power tools cost about 500 to 600 Euros, which shouldn't break the bank.

However, the first and most important consideration is the owner himself. He or she must derive pleasure from doing the work itself, otherwise the entire project will be one long slog. Anyone who doesn't actually enjoy this kind of work should consider doing something else. If you don't enjoy working on boats, the chances are you'll probably give up half way through. Remember, refitting a yacht is an all-consuming and complex undertaking.

On the other hand, some people enjoy the work. For them, this is a hobby – and something they really like doing. Difficulties, which will undoubtedly occur, are merely seen as interesting challenges. They also realise that when things go wrong, that's the best way to learn. And even if their backs ache after a long day working on the boat, most of them will tell you it was great fun.

To make sure your project is a success, and to make sure you enjoy every stage of it, there are three golden rules in my book.

Number One: It's all or nothing. With a proper refit you have to go all the way. Anyone who starts cutting corners half way through or even begins with the intention of refitting only parts of the boat will run into big problems later on. A half-hearted approach like this will never enhance the value of the boat. Badly refitted boats are difficult if not virtually impossible to sell – particularly if botched attempts have really messed things up and made them worse than they were to start with.

Number Two: Always proceed on a step-by-step basis. Finish one job before beginning the next. Working on too many things at the same time will inevitably lead to chaos and eventual abandonment. Tackling the exterior hull, the water systems and the boat's electrical installation all at once will soon cause a lack of focus. It's all too easy to lose sight of the really important aspects of the refit. Always concentrate on one aspect of the project, finish it, and enjoy the sense of pride and satisfaction it gives you, before embarking on the next.

Number Three: plan, plan and plan. Sensible overall planning of the complete refit is one of the keys to eventual success; that's why I've devoted the next chapter to it. Using a fibreglass boat as an example, we shall system-atically work through all the necessary planning stages and draw up a list of priorities.

Whether you decide to do up a fibreglass or a wooden boat depends on several consider-ations. Fibreglass generally requires less specialist knowledge than wood, so that might be the better choice for the DIY beginner. Since fibreglass has a long life, regular maintenance after the refit will be limited to simple cosmetic measures like cleaning and polishing. Wooden boats on the other hand require considerably more work and attention. Here's just one example: if water or excess humidity has crept underneath your varnish, it means scraping back to bare wood and re-varnishing. However, working on a wooden boat can be highly satisfying in itself and the general ambience of timber is hard to match; fibreglass, in comparison, is functional but far less aesthetic.

In the first part of the book, we consider the kind of work you might do on a typical fibreglass cruiser; our guinea-pig is an Avance 24. In the second half, we describe how we refitted a plywood-built Waarschip 570. These particular boats have one thing in common; both are very popular (in Europe, at least) and should fetch good prices after their refits.

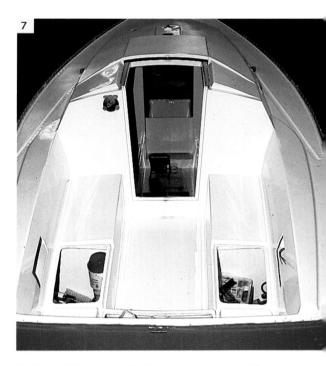

7 After all the work she's as good as new. The finished cockpit looks absolutely immaculate.

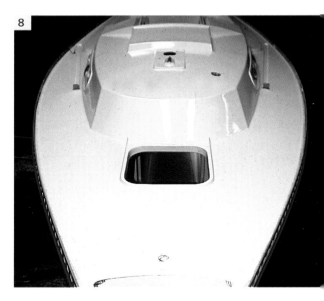

8 Almost perfect. A shot of a beautifully restored deck that belies the boat's 25 years.

9 Professional advice saves time and money.

If you have complex or specific questions about particular aspects of the refit, you can always seek the advice of a professional surveyor. Do make sure however that the surveyor you contact does indeed specialise in your type of boat – particularly as far as the construction is concerned. Another extremely good source of information and helpful hints and tips are the various class and owners' associations that exist for many popular types of boat.

The photos in this chapter show how we prepared for the refit of our 24 footer.

CHECKLIST

Ship's documents
- Bill of sale: OK?
- VAT status: paid?
- How many previous owners?
- Owner's manuals available?

Rigging
- Mast, mast step, cross-trees
- Main boom, gooseneck
- Spinnaker pole, kicking strap
- Standing rigging
- Running rigging
- Condition of timber or alloy spars
- Aerials
- Navigation lights
- Windex or wind indicator
- Blocks and fittings

Sailing characteristics
- Test sail in at least F4 to 5
- Helm and handling characteristics
- Sheets and winches
- Sail trim
- Watertight?
- Movement of bulkheads etc?
- Condition of all the sails

Engine characteristics
- Impressions of engine/installation
- Engine mounts

- Cold starting
- Power
- Vibration
- Exhaust fumes, cooling water
- Gears and transmission
- Propeller
- Spark plugs
- Not sure? Ask a specialist

Hull
- Check underwater sections
- Osmosis? Cracks in the gel coat?
- Surfaces: scratches, cracks?
- Rudder hangings
- Keel/hull joint
- Speedo, echo sounder
- Sea-cocks, corrosion
- Antifouling: too many layers?

Interior
- Damp? Smelly?
- Water in the bilges?
- Leaking windows or hatches?
- Electrical installation/batteries
- Cooker, stove
- Heating and ventilation
- Stowage space
- Toilet
- Plumbing, water tanks

THE FIBREGLASS YACHT

How to plan the refit

How careful planning, right from the start, will help prevent mistakes and save you time and money later on. How, also, to organise the preparation efficiently.

Let's suppose you've either found a boat which needs a refit, or you want to restore the one you already own. You're probably itching to roll your sleeves up and start work straight away. However, it's important to make a careful assessment of the situation and all the work to be done before you actually begin.

In fact, you should be as enthusiastic about making a detailed plan as painting the hull or polishing the gel coat later on. Otherwise, you might find you've completed the interior before treating the bilge to a last coat of paint. With proper planning, one step will inevitably lead to another and the stages of the project will fit together and complement each other perfectly.

Before you can actually draw up a plan though, you should take stock of the boat and its condition. After that you should make a list of everything that needs to be replaced or refurbished, section by section. Using a laptop

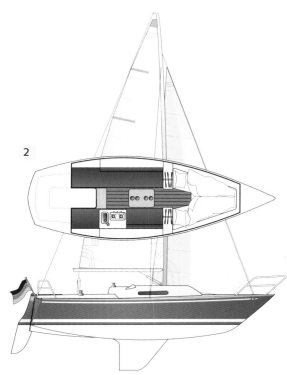

2

1 The Avance 24, shown here before the refit.

2 Spec: LOA, 7.46 m; LWL, 6 m; Beam, 2.54 m, Draft, 1.45 m; Displacement, 1.9 tons; Sail area, 30 square metres; Construction, glass reinforced plastic (fibreglass).

3 This is how the boat shaped up after the refit. As you can see in this picture, she's nearly ready.

computer will help enormously at this stage, because it's so easy to make amendments. If you don't have a laptop, write everything down in note-form and type it into your PC at home. You might think this all sounds rather complicated, but it really does make a difference if you begin with a sensible plan. It also helps with the financial side, so you can keep to your budget. Once you've made a list of all the various stages, it's not difficult to find out the prices of equipment and replacement parts you're likely to need, using

3

4 It's far better to buy good tools and save on quantity rather than quality. For a project like this, a fairly basic kit might include the following: two sets of different sized screwdrivers, Allen keys of various sizes, spanners, various pliers (snub, long-nosed etc), a bolt cutter, hammers, high quality drill bits for steel and wood, plug cutters, metal saws, ten screw cramps, and an assortment of files. As you can see, it's not a huge amount of kit but, even so, will get you quite a long way. As for power tools, the most obvious ones you might need would include a drill, screwdriver, jig saw, sanding machine and an industrial quality vacuum cleaner.

5 However tempted you might be, don't try to stow anything inside the boat. If you do, something will always get in the way and make the job a lot harder. Instead, remove every single piece of equipment, clean it, label it and stow it in a dry and secure place. Tanks should be emptied before you stow them away in your garage or shed. You can also keep your gas bottles here; remember, for safety's sake, you should never leave them inside your house.

6 Making simple and inexpensive shelving like this is a good way of creating storage space in your garage or workshop. In this particular example, two shallow shelves have been screwed to one another to give extra depth to accommodate tools and building materials.

chandlers' catalogues or by browsing their Internet pages. And remember: don't hesitate to ask for special rates when buying large quantities of equipment or materials. By the same token, it's worth trying to order everything from one source provided, of course, that in doing so, you do indeed qualify for substantial discounts.

And here's another tip while you're still at the planning stage: a picture says more than

7 It's easy to get confused if you remove items and just put them casually aside somewhere. Everything you remove or dismantle should be listed and labelled. This is also the time to decide what can be used again and what needs to be replaced.

8 Bilges often hide a multitude of problems on older boats. Take up the floorboards, and the chances are you'll see rusty bolts and scruffy surfaces. Check the keel bolts, remove the nuts and replace them with new ones if rusty.

9 As a rule it's best to change and renew all rubber or plastic hoses whatever they may be used for (freshwater, toilet, bilgewater). They all become porous in time and are then likely to break and leak. When replacing them, choose spiralled hoses that won't get blocked when bent into tight corners and radiuses.

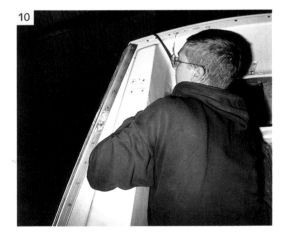

10 When dismantling again, label everything and put the fastenings back into the fittings after having taken them off the boat. That way, you won't have to look for the right screw, bolt, or nut or even buy new ones when it's time to put them back on again. Dismantling is best done with a team of two: one above and one below decks. Stainless steel should be polished before you put it back on the boat.

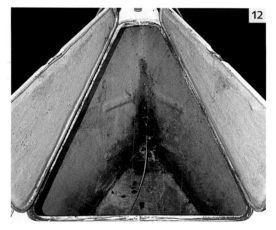

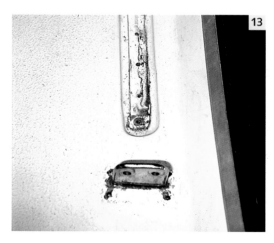

11 The outboard bracket can be overhauled at home. This is a good way to fill the time when you can't work on the boat, for example when you're waiting for layers of paint to dry. Also have a good look at the state of the fibreglass where the bracket is attached to the boat. It may need to be reinforced with a layer or two of new laminate on the inside of the boat.

12 Remove the hatch of the anchor locker on the foredeck. They often sustain damage because of the high mechanical stresses encountered here. Before filling or painting, clean the surfaces thoroughly. Anchor lockers are also often used as storage for fuel canisters, which often deposit a film of oil on the inside. Use heavy-duty paint for the interior of the locker.

13 Remove the genoa sheet tracks and chainplate covers. Sometimes, genoa track bolts are different lengths to accommodate different deck thickness, so put them back into the track in the right order, once the track is removed, and secure the bolts with nuts.

a thousand words. That's why any good refit is best documented step-by-step, with photographs or sketches showing the 'before' and 'after' effects. It's not only personally satisfying to make a record like this, but also helps immensely if the boat should be subsequently sold. Nothing provides better proof that the relevant work has actually been undertaken than a file full of pictures.

A rough estimate of the time scale involved is also an essential part of the overall plan. You want to know how long each stage of the restoration should take and when it might be finished. Try and estimate a realistic time-frame within an accuracy of, say, a week. Otherwise, it's easy to lose sight of the overall picture and how far you've got with the project. After all, however much you

14 This substantial damage to the toe-rail only came to light after it was taken apart. Using aluminium for the rail and stainless stanchion bases is less than ideal. The aluminium has corroded quite deeply. These areas should be thoroughly cleaned and then painted with a coat of protective paint. This is also an opportunity to tighten up all the toe-rail bolts.

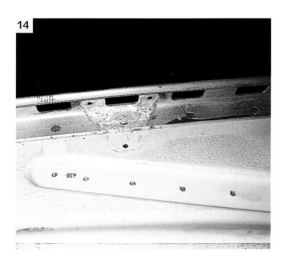

15 Components and fittings like the mast step on deck can quite easily be covered with masking tape allowing you to later paint round it, so you don't have to dismantle it or take it off. On the other hand, protruding fittings should always be removed as a matter of course, because it's far less easy to paint round them.

16 Remove all fittings such as winches, clutches and sheet stoppers. Before you take them off or dismantle them though, take a few photographs or make a sketch if you plan to keep the same deck layout, to show where everything goes. Hardware like this can be stowed at home, where it can be cleaned and greased at your leisure, when you have time.

enjoy doing the refit, at some stage, you'll want to finish it and go sailing!

If you need to complete everything and get afloat at the beginning of the new season, say in the spring, you might, for example, have to begin the whole operation the year before, perhaps in August. That would give you enough time to look around on the market, find suitable boats and still test sail them before their owners laid them up for the winter. Make sure you have a professional survey, and at the same time, find a suitable place to carry out the work. Many owners who want to trade in their old boats for newer or larger ones often don't want to be bothered any more with storing them away for the winter, so there's a good chance of picking up a bargain.

17 Once the deck fittings have been removed, you'll be surprised at the number of holes left in the deck. Many yards use silicone paste to make them watertight, but you can't paint over the top of it. You'll have to remove it all by drilling it out of the apertures, then cleaning everything with special thinners.

18 If you don't plan on using any of the holes again, because, for example, old fittings are to be replaced with new ones, then you should clearly mark where they all are. Drill out the silicone, then clean and fill with good quality filler, and sand down.

19 This interior lining is beyond repair and has to come off. It's deteriorated and torn in places. Not only that, mildew often forms behind damaged linings like this, so it's a real problem. There's nothing you can do except remove the old lining completely, clean the interior surface of the deckhead and put a new lining back on in its place.

Let's begin with a look at the rigging. How much of it can be saved, and what needs to be replaced? Jot down all the lengths and diameters of the standing and running rigging, as well as the type of spars and the name of the manufacturer. This will save time later, when ordering new bits and pieces at the sailmaker or rigger.

After having checked the rigging and sails, take a close look at the outboard. Does it need an overhaul? To find out, inspect it thoroughly, and give it a proper test run. Again, make a note of the make, type and serial number, as well as the size and pitch of propeller and so on.

Remove all the layers of old paint from the hull. If the hull is made of fibreglass, are there signs of osmosis? If it's a wooden boat, is any of the timber soft or rotten? What about the joint between the keel and hull? Is the seam sound, and insulated with rubber, or are there rust streaks that require further investigation

20 All the items will have to be removed from every surface you want to paint or varnish. On older boats, a clear varnish may not really be a practical option particularly if numerous things have been mounted and dismantled over the years. It will always look worn and discoloured. If that's the case, a nice coat of new paint is a far better solution.

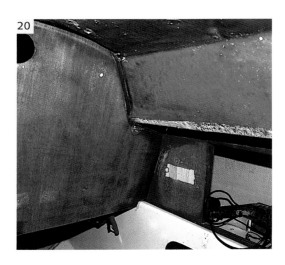

21 Fibreglass tanks which have been laminated into the boat, probably at the building stage, can be left in position and cleaned assuming, of course, that they have large enough diameter inspection hatches to provide the access you need. The hoses will probably be replaced anyway.

22 Ancient radios, lights, coat hooks and the like should all be removed and thrown away. Don't keep anything you don't need. The cut-outs in the bulkheads can be sealed with plywood, the edges then filled with epoxy filler and sanded down. After that, apply a coat of primer before painting.

and treatment? What does the rudder look like? Are there any signs of a grounding? What sort of condition are the bearings in? Is there any water dripping from it or is the shaft slightly bent?

Lead keels don't usually cause any problems. But iron keels should be sanded off and coated with a fresh layer of rust preventive paint. Antifouling would be applied as the very last layer. Now for the hull: are there any damaged areas that need to be filled or repaired? Or, on a wooden boat, do any planks need replacing? Inspect the topsides closely and mark any problem areas with a felt-tip pen. Then proceed to the deck. For a thorough refit, all the fittings need to be removed. Apply the same degree of care and dedication to the interior. Make a note of anything that needs to be replaced or repaired under different headings, for example: wood/joinery, bilge, electrical installation, plumbing, lining, upholstery and windows/hatches etc.

Underwater sections and bilges

With the planning completed and everything fully prepared, you can now start work on the bottom of the boat – both inside and out. This is the best way to tackle the sanding, filling and painting.

Admittedly, it's not much fun working on your back for hours on end, wearing a protective mask, wielding heavy sanding machines or beavering away with paint scrapers. Your arms soon get heavy; there are healthier environments too. However, nothing's more important than making sure

the bottom of the boat is in really good shape. Keel, hull, rudder and bilges – these components are the core or backbone of any yacht, and form the foundations on which every successful refit is built. These are tough jobs, but once you've done them, and done them thoroughly and well, you're on firm ground and can press on with the rest of the refit, knowing you've completed one of the most demanding parts of the entire project.

Before applying new paint, make perfectly sure that the boat is free of osmosis which often appears on boats around 20 to 25 years old. To diagnose the problem, look for small bubbles or blisters underneath the last layer of paint, especially if, when punctured, they release an acid-like and evil smelling liquid. (Remember to protect your eyes!) If you're not sure, consult a surveyor who will be able to measure the amount of moisture in the laminate. The boat we've used as an example here turned out to be healthy in this respect. But even if your boat has osmosis, it's not the end of the world. In the early days, it caused panic but these days, we're more relaxed about the problem because we know it can be treated and cured. On the other hand, even if your boat is sound now, a layer of osmosis-preventive paint will help make sure that it stays that way in the future. Indeed, it always makes sense to apply a coating like this when you undertake a complete refit.

First, all the old paint must come off. That takes time and effort and you should allow about 35 hours to complete this job alone. How it can best be done is described in the following sequence. The photos show an osmosis preventive system, treating the keel and rudder, filling holes and coating the bilges. But first, let's start with the essential tools.

A: Off with the old paint. Use a scraper like this, with blades that can be changed, and a fitting which connects to a vacuum cleaner.

B: A heavy duty vacuum cleaner swallows all the old paint dust and flakes if connected to the scraper. It also helps keep the air cleaner.

C: Getting into all the nooks and crannies. This rotating nylon brush is useful and will help clean away left over bits of paint and rust.

D: Orbital sander. No good for removing soft antifouling paint; the paper quickly clogs up. However, it's OK for sanding the gelcoat.

E: Waterproof fillers. Use a two pot product like this, which can even be used underwater. Only prepare small amounts at a time.

F: Cleaning up on the inside. It's best to use a good quality, purpose made bilge paint which is tough, flexible and easy to apply.

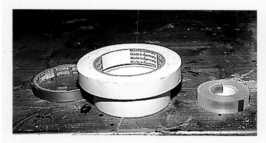

G: Essentials: you simply can't do without masking tape. Larger areas can be covered with film, but always fix the edges with masking tape.

H: Use a tray. You should never use paint directly from the can. If you're using a foam roller you really need a tray.

1 You should always cover the keel with a protective plastic skirt like this before removing the old paint. It helps keep the air inside the shed clean. Another must: for safety's sake, you should also wear a protective mask over your face. Finally, as another precaution, your scraping tool should be connected to a vacuum cleaner so only the minimum amount of old paint will be released into the air or settle on the ground.

2 Scraping off the paint requires strength as well as concentration. It's sensible to change the blades fairly frequently; working with blunt blades only makes the job more difficult. But be extremely careful not to tilt the scraper. Even if it's canted over only slightly, you'll leave deep gouges in the gelcoat. Take a break every half hour or so – otherwise you'll get tired and make mistakes.

3 A good rotary sander helps a lot, as soon as you start removing hard layers of paint. But when dealing with soft layers of antifouling, the paper will clog up extremely quickly. To reduce friction and avoid unnecessary heating up of the surface when sanding, don't apply too much pressure.

4 Rounded areas and hollows can only be sanded by hand. Start with 40 Grade paper, then use 80 Grade and finish off with 120. Only lightly sand the gelcoat. Always try to have proper lighting.

5 Never completely remove the original boot top because putting on a new line takes a lot of effort, time and patience. If you're changing the width or height of the boot top, mark the new line with a waterproof felt tip pen at regular intervals, then draw a line using a long bendy batten.

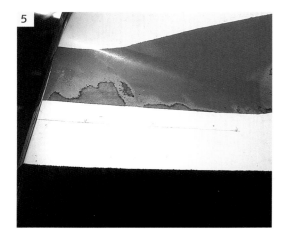

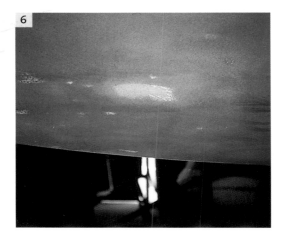

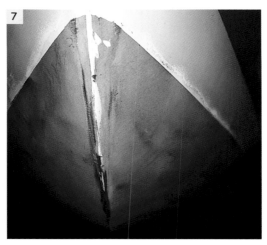

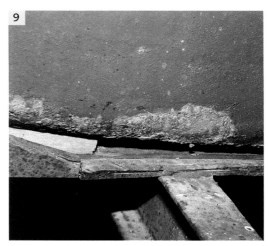

6 This can happen quickly. A momentary lapse of concentration, bad lighting or rough sanding paper, and suddenly the gelcoat has been damaged so the fibres of the laminate show through. It's not a disaster, but you should always try to make sure the protective gelcoat stays intact.

7 Try to leave as much of the gelcoat on the boat as possible. It's not always possible, especially if the hull is unsound or when removing blisters. Damaged areas should be filled with waterproof two-pot filler, then sanded down. The laminate underneath must be dry and clean.

8 When you've finished all the scraping and sanding, cover the boot top with masking tape, support the boat and lower away the trailer supports. Clean the bottom thoroughly with a special detergent, then apply the osmosis barrier with a foam roller. Now, the underwater area has been protected; the final layer of antifouling can follow in the spring.

9 The older the boat, the more rust will appear on the keel, especially if it's made of cast iron. Areas that are exposed to mechanical stresses will suffer most. The bottom of the keel will also have rust if the paint here has been damaged.

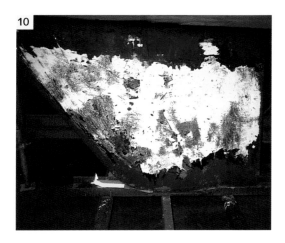

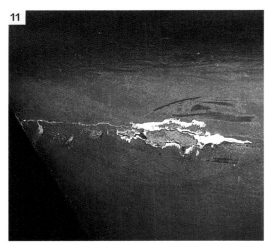

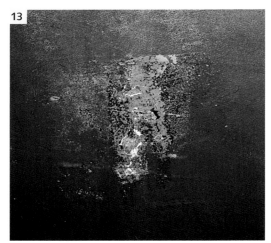

10 The surface here has been cleaned of rust and now simply needs to be faired with a filler, then sanded down. As a rule, only use epoxy filler below the water line. After sanding, two to three coats of osmosis protective paint can be applied per day, without the need for any more sanding in between.

11 Stresses are particularly high at the joint between keel and hull. Cracks are also likely to develop because of the different thermal expansion characteristics of the materials. For that reason, never fill the gaps with rigid filler or laminate. Use a flexible, silicone-free rubber sealant.

12 This seal between the fibreglass hull and the keel is still completely sound. After a light sanding, it can be painted straight away. Good quality primers and undercoats can be applied to both fibreglass and steel, so you don't need two different paint systems here.

13 Examine the keel closely to track down every source of rust. Expose the areas that cause concern, remove all traces of corrosion and apply a suitable primer. If the keel has suffered a lot, it may be necessary to sandblast and build up a completely new paint system which includes a good rust preventative.

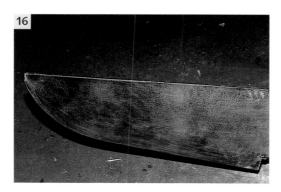

15 If it's absolutely impossible to stick to the manufacturer's recommended time intervals between each layer of paint there's only one course of action: you must laboriously sand again between coats. Follow the instructions closely so you don't make more work for yourself. Remember that any manufacturer's guarantee will be invalid if you don't follow the instructions.

16 A rudder blade made of fibreglass is also subject to possible osmosis. That's why you need to treat it the same way as the hull. First remove all the old paint, then fill the cracks and blisters, sand down and finally apply six coats of osmosis barrier paint.

17 This is how to enlarge a hole in the hull. It's something you have to do before filling it – and would be necessary after you removed a skin fitting which you'd decided not to replace, for example. Start by using a rough file to prepare the edges. Take them back substantially and don't be afraid to leave the surfaces of the edges rough to provide a good base for the filler.

18 A metal blade, wrapped in plastic, should then be taped against the hole from the outside. Epoxy resin won't bond with the PVC so, for that reason, after it's cured, you get a fairly smooth surface – which will then only have to be lightly sanded before you finally paint it.

19 Three to four layers of glassfibre mat is usually sufficient to cover a hole of about 15 centimetres in diameter. However, the larger the hole, of course, the more layers you'll need. Always use a good sharp knife to cut the mats into the desired shape.

14 The osmosis barrier can be applied with a brush or a roller. If you use a foam roller, you'll need two rollers per layer. That makes twelve rollers for six coats of paint. The rollers are simply thrown away after use so you don't need to bother with cleaning them.

20 Fill the hole with the epoxy resin-hardener mix. Then push the glassfibre mat into the hole with a small brush. Next, you should slowly add resin until the fibres become transparent. Alternatively, you could also use glassfibre filler to fill the hole.

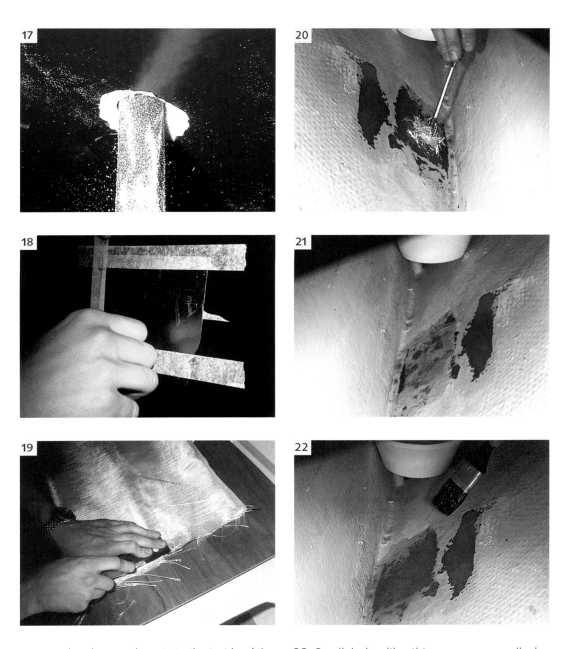

21 Use a brush to apply resin to the inside of the hull around the hole. This whole area has been thoroughly cleaned beforehand to ensure a really good bond. You should apply one glassfibre mat, then saturate it with resin, and carefully add the next layers.

22 Small holes like this one can usually be covered with three layers, though, of course, larger diameter holes would need more. You should always apply each of the layers while the resin is still wet, so they adhere together and form a proper bond. Always use epoxy resin.

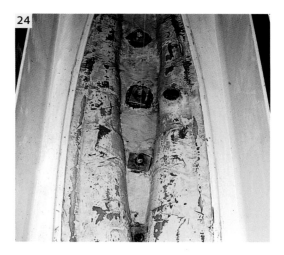

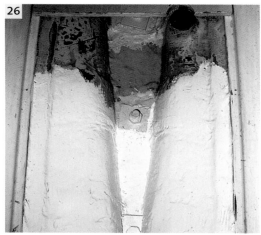

23 Bilges which are covered with permanently screwed down floor-boards can hide big corrosion problems. Take the nuts off the keel bolts and check if the bolts themselves are still free of rust and in a satisfactory condition. In most cases everything should be OK because the bolts themselves are seldom affected − but you can't be too careful.

24 Before putting the nuts back on, clean them thoroughly, removing any rust, or use new ones. Use a silicone-free sealant underneath the washers. Tighten the nuts only lightly. Once the sealant has cured about a day later, tighten the nuts completely.

25 Nuts, bolts and washers should be treated with a good quality rust protective paint, which, in my view, should preferably be of the two-pot epoxy type. It's always best to apply at least two or three coats. The surrounding fibreglass surfaces should have been sanded and cleaned in advance, of course.

26 Apply a heavy duty bilge paint directly to the fibreglass surface. Again, two to three coats are needed. If the fibreglass has been sanded until the fibres are exposed, a suitable undercoat should be applied first to keep the water out and help prevent wicking.

Painting the hull and deck

This stage of the operation is a real challenge: painting the hull, deck and cockpit by hand, with just a brush and a roller.

1 Whether you're using the roller or the brush, remember this job requires care and control.

Even the best maintained topsides may look a bit scruffy after 20 or 30 years. UV-rays, air pollution, salt water and hundreds of scratches, large and small, will inevitably affect the appearance of the gelcoat; the surface loses its shine and looks dull. Clearly, it's time for a new coat of paint, which you can apply with just a brush and a roller.

If the gelcoat is still between about 0.3 and 0.5 millimetres thick, you might get away without a paint job at all. In that case, a thorough polish might be enough to restore

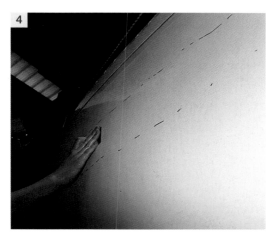

it to at least some of its former glory. However, thinner gelcoats will definitely need painting. Having said that, polishing is only worthwhile if the hull is mainly free of scratches, blisters or other signs of damage. Otherwise, you might as well forget about it. And local or minor repairs will always show up because it's almost impossible to accurately match the colour of the gelcoat. The results usually stand out like a sore thumb.

In the case of our 25-year-old Avance, I decided on a completely new coat of paint for two reasons: on the one hand, I wanted to get rid of the numerous dents in the hull which, as it happens, were there from the day she was launched, as well as the hundreds of scratches which had accumulated over the years. On the other hand, I also wanted to change the colour of the hull, in the hope that the boat would look more up to date.

2 Orbital sanding machines like this should be used only on straight and slightly curved areas. Connect it up to a vacuum cleaner and always wear a protective mask. Use 240 Grade paper or something finer for the intermediate sanding between coats as well as for the first rub-down.

3 Sanding by hand is incredibly exhausting, but gives the best results. Wear gloves to protect your hands and try wrapping the sand paper round a cork block to make it easier to handle. Don't apply too much pressure, and change the paper as soon as it begins to clog with dust.

4 Uneven parts and small defects in the hull can best be seen before the topsides are sanded. Look up along the topsides from the waterline and mark all the areas that need to be repaired with a felt-tip pen. Take care when filling cracks and small dents. If you're too generous with the filler, you'll have to do a lot of additional sanding later on.

Not everyone has enough confidence to take on this job alone. If you're personally undecided, remember, you can still save money by splitting the operation in two – doing the first phase yourself and leaving the rest to professionals. All the time-consuming preparation, like dismantling the fittings and masking the windows and toe-rail, as well as the cleaning and sanding of the hull with 320 Grade paper can be done by the owners and their friends. The paint job itself can then be carried out by the experts.

However, if you also want to paint the boat yourself, there are two alternatives. One is to use a simple, one pot paint which is easy to apply, runs more smoothly and is less sensitive to the temperature. On the downside, the end result won't be as hard and durable as the two-pot alternative – which, once it's dried out completely, will be nearly as hard as the gelcoat. If you're using

5 Epoxy filler lets you fill up dents to a thickness of about 15 millimetres. Don't apply it all at once; it's better to do it in layers. A steel ruler can then be used to remove excess filler. The pot-life of epoxy filler is around 20 minutes in 15 degrees Celsius.

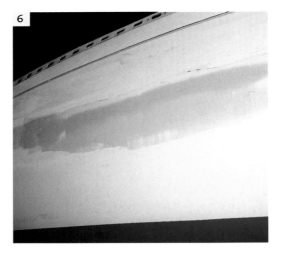

6 Epoxy bonds extremely well to glassfibre and when dry, becomes very hard. It might be hard to sand down at that stage, so again, be as accurate as possible when filling. It's better to use a little less epoxy at first, even if you have to apply a second layer, than to use too much and sand it all down again later. Small cracks can be treated with polyester-filler.

7 Large dents should be filled with epoxy filler and faired. If small holes or uneven areas remain, you can also fill them with polyester filler, which is easier to sand down afterwards. Take care not to leave air bubbles in the filler. They turn into small craters when sanded.

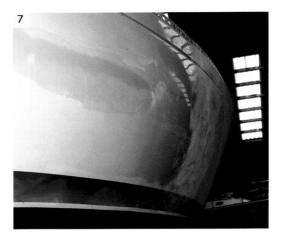

a two-pot paint for the first time, I would suggest you try it out on a small area first to get used to the flow characteristics and hardening times.

But before we begin, we'll have to remove all the fittings – winches, genoa tracks, traveller, cleats and so on. The next step is to clean the gelcoat with acetone to remove any traces of grease. Give it a good rub down, then fill and fair where necessary and finally sand with a very fine, 320-Grade paper. If silicone has been used anywhere on the hull or deck as a sealant, it would have to be removed completely because the paint won't stick to it. When rubbing down and sanding, make absolutely sure that none of the silicone sticks to the sanding paper, otherwise you'll spread it all over the hull! One-pot systems can be made compatible with silicone by mixing a special additive with the paint.

Once the surface is smooth and all traces of dust have been removed using special dust absorbing tissue (available in DIY stores), the primer can be applied. You'll need two or three coats. The next step is to apply three or four coats of topcoat. Continue painting until the colour is even all over.

It's important to follow the manufacturer's instructions. And before applying the final coat of paint, sand down with wet 320-Grade paper to remove any traces of brush lines. The

8 The last fine layer of filling can be done with a normal filler designed for use above the water line. It can be applied thinly with a metal blade. Mix the filler on a small piece of plywood then pick up small amounts with the blade. This kind of filler can easily be sanded afterwards.

9 In the course of the refit, you might not want to put back some of the old fittings. If so, clean the holes from all old sealant, enlarge the edges of the hole, wash and clean with thinners to remove silicone traces and fill with filler. Fair and sand afterwards.

10 The two halves of the hull weren't joined very neatly during the original building process. The result is an uneven seam at the stem. The visual effect can be improved during the refit. Sand down, fill where necessary, and paint, along with the topsides. Take care that the seam is well covered with paint, otherwise there's a danger that water might get in later on.

pot life obviously depends on the surrounding temperature. In 5 degrees Celsius it will be five hours, in 15 degrees Celsius three hours and in 23 degrees Celsius only two hours. As a rough guide to how much paint you might need, about 750 millilitres should be enough for one coat on a 24-foot boat and can easily be applied in three hours. But if you find it takes longer, remember the golden rule: you should never use the paint beyond the manufacturer's estimated pot life. If you do, the paint simply won't flow anymore and might even look dull when it dries.

In hot climates, only paint one side of the hull at a time, then use fresh paint for the other side. Use thinners with the paint but only according to the manufacturer's instructions. Always apply the paint with the roller first, then fair it with the brush immediately afterwards. Note that if you use two-pot paints, they also need two-pot primers.

You'll get the best results if you rub down between coats with a fine, 240-Grade paper for the primers and 320-Grade paper for the topcoats. You should do the jobs in the following order: start off by masking the boot top, windows, toe-rail and any remaining fittings with tape. After that, apply the primer to the deck and coachroof, then paint white topcoat on the deck. Next, apply two or three coats of paint to the hull. The white boot top stripe should be painted last of all.

11 Sometimes, when masking off sharp edges, tape may not be the best solution. Cling film might be more suitable – but, if possible, try not to use the transparent variety. Tape can be stuck over the film afterwards. Remove all the masking tape and film as quickly as possible after painting; don't leave it too long.

12 If the window frames weren't removed, mask the edges with cling film and support with tape. Again remove as quickly as possible after painting.

Film and tape stick to aluminium with a vengeance and if you wait for a couple of days, both can become near impossible to remove.

13 Prime the hull until the colour is even. You might well have to apply two to three layers of primer. Then apply the paint. Always use both hands. Apply the paint with the roller in one hand and fair with the brush immediately afterwards with the other. I used four 750 millilitre cans for the hull and deck of my boat.

14 It's best to keep to the original waterline or boot top because at least it should be straight. If you have to modify it, mark the waterline with a long flexible batten, around six metres long. You'll need at least four people to hold it in place. Mark with a felt-tip, then mask the edges. Prime and paint in the same way as you did with the topsides.

15 After the entire surface has been carefully cleaned of dust with a special moist, dust-removing cloth, wash your hands etc and begin painting, using a roller and brush. Always paint small surfaces one at a time. Each section should be no larger than roughly half a square metre.

16 After applying two or three layers, it's time for the final coat. Here, with a boat like this, you might need three tins for the deck. Remember to rub down with wet sandpaper before the final coat. If you happen to find any insects trapped in the wet paint, don't panic; you can leave them until the paint has completely dried, then carefully polish them away afterwards.

17 The transom-hung rudder should be painted at the same time as the topsides. If you don't do this, you might have problems matching the colour. Before you begin it's a good idea to lash the rudder blade so that it doesn't move but can be painted from both sides in one go.

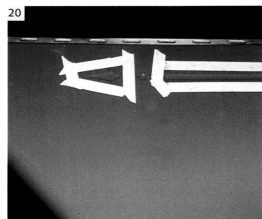

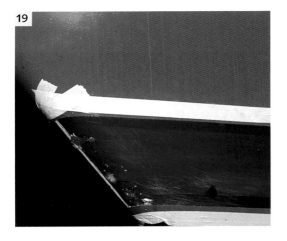

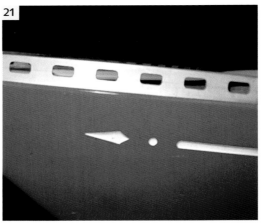

18 Careful masking with tape or film is one of the most important parts of the preparation. If the masking is unsatisfactory, the final paint job will be too. When you want to make a new edge which needs to be masked, it's always best to first draw a line with a felt-tip pen so you have something to line up against. But don't stretch the film; it only makes the edges uneven.

19 If the masking tape isn't very wide, it's not really much of a problem; you can always use two overlapping layers. Remember, though, that foam rollers need quite a wide area of overlap along the edges. Don't forget to clean the surfaces well before applying the tape.

20 The thin strip or cove line along the upper topside is an important decorative feature but a fairly tricky item to mask and paint. If you don't want to bother with it, simply paint the topsides and later use one of those adhesive decorating strips available from chandlers. As well as a range of different colours, they can also be had in gold or silver.

21 After priming, you then follow up with three to four layers of paint on top. For the final coat, you should always use a new set of rollers and brushes. For the intermediate coats, you can clean your brushes with thinners – but, of course, they'll never be as good as new.

Refurbishing below decks

Dark wooden panelling can look claustrophobic, but you can brighten it up by using white or light colours, leaving a little wood trim for an authentic boaty feel.

To begin with, you'll have to take almost everything out. So lights, clock, barometer, coat hooks, loudspeakers, radio and switchpanel – all must be removed. This is also the time to think about the things you

1 The open bulkheads between the saloon and the forepeak can be solid at the bottom and have a door in the upper part (see also the chapter 'Fitting lockers and frames').

2 Dismantling: as we've already suggested, it's a good idea to remove all the fittings before starting to paint.

3 Over the years, this chainplate attachment has worked loose from its fibreglass base on the side of the hull. It goes without saying that this is a vitally important component which must cope with very high forces and on which the whole safety of the boat could depend. To begin a repair like this, first expose the critical area as much as possible.

4 We made use of wooden wedges to force the

fitting and the fibreglass base even further apart so the surface could be sanded. To add extra strength, we drilled three holes to take some M6/M8 stainless steel bolts then mixed some epoxy resin with a thickening additive and applied generously before inserting the bolts and tightening.

5 After the epoxy has cured, we had to tighten the bolts again and cut off any excess thread with a bolt cutter or sharp hacksaw. We also smoothed the ends of the bolts with a file to minimise the risk of injury.

6 Now was the time to replace the original wooden cladding, then sand and varnish it. It's best to fit cladding like this in place with screws to make it easier to remove and provide access should the need arise later on. It's preferable to gluing.

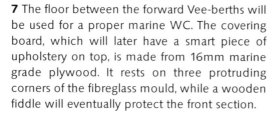

7 The floor between the forward Vee-berths will be used for a proper marine WC. The covering board, which will later have a smart piece of upholstery on top, is made from 16mm marine grade plywood. It rests on three protruding corners of the fibreglass mould, while a wooden fiddle will eventually protect the front section.

8 Gluing in a small bulkhead between the forward Vee-berths. We used epoxy to bond it in place. In fact, it's primary function will simply be to hide most of the WC from view later on. In a case like this, it's advisable to leave a reasonable gap along the bottom to stop water from collecting in such a confined area.

might want to change. For example you might be thinking about new locker lids or adding some mahogany trim to some of the furniture. Again, it helps if you draw up a detailed plan of campaign. Once the interior has been more or less stripped, many fittings which are otherwise difficult to get to, will be exposed. So take this opportunity to check the hull-deck joint from the inside and tighten up any loose bolts on the toe-rail. And don't forget to check all the other through-deck fittings like handrails, hatches and vents to make sure that all are secure and won't leak. Only then should you begin tackling the actual woodwork.

You should also check to see if the chain-plates are still secure. These fittings are subject to high forces and can come loose over a period

of time. In our case, the laminate between the fibreglass and the chain-plate had deteriorated and had to be renewed. We also renewed all the wardrobe and locker doors and replaced them with white ones, which have an attractive, wooden trim around the edges.

You should also make a check-list of all your wood-working requirements. How many doors will be replaced? Which lockers or shelves can remain open? How big should the doors actually be?

The general rule here is as big as necessary and as small as possible. In real life, very large doors are simply impractical on board when you have people moving about because they need a lot of room to open. On our Avance, we secured each of the large rectangular

9 After fitting this miniature bulkhead, we had to fill the sides and sand everything smooth for the final finish. The underside of the plywood itself has already been protected with epoxy. This is absolutely vital and we did it in advance because, of course, it's impossible to varnish it once it's been fitted.

10 The paint here has been used mainly as a barrier against moisture. You should sand down all the wood and fibreglass surfaces, then clean and apply two coats of primer. After that, you might apply two coats of two-pot polyurethane paint. This provides good protection and looks smart.

stowage bins with two separate doors so they could be opened one at a time, which helps prevent things from falling out at sea.

Once you've decided on the number and sizes of the doors, you need to make even more lists. This is especially important when working out the lengths of the battens to cover up the edges. Make sure you total up all the edges and buy enough battens in one go, otherwise the next strips will be from another tree and will never match the exact colour or grain of the first set and can ruin the whole effect.

By the same token, it's far better to end up with a metre or so too much, than a metre too little, and don't forget that you can also make mistakes when cutting the battens to size. This can happen more easily than you might

imagine, so be careful. Just two millimetres too short can mean you have to re-cut an entire new batten. For that reason, always begin by cutting the long strips first – if anything goes wrong here, you can use them to cut the shorter ones later.

Invest in proper tools too, because they make life so much easier and really earn their keep. And work carefully and to precise measurements. If, for example, the gaps between door and surrounding bulkhead aren't exactly parallel to each other and differ in width, it ruins the look of the whole job. Don't settle for second best. In this case, the door should be thrown away and a new one made. Otherwise, you will always be angry every time you see it later.

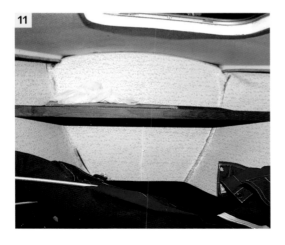

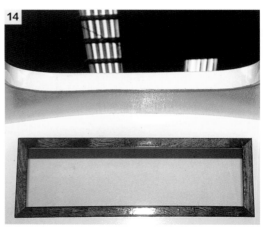

11 To use more of the available space in the forepeak, you could always fit a large stowage shelf above the forward end of the berths. The yard originally only fitted a single flat shelf with a small fiddle, which neither looked very good nor was particularly practical. However, we've used the original shelf as a basis for a new, improved version which is infinitely more practical.

12 Before fitting the new storage space, the entire forepeak had to be emptied and the cladding or lining removed. If you're planning a job like this, remember, it can be a fairly long job, depending on the quality of the glue that was originally used.

13 You don't necessarily have to close off athwartship storage with a door or hatch, of course. The opening should, however, incorporate some form of high fiddle at the bottom to prevent things from falling out in heavy weather at sea. Here, as you can see, the previously cut-to-fit front panel has now been securely glued in with epoxy.

14 Gluing a varnished mahogany frame into the opening. The idea here was that it should blend in naturally with the rest of the decor. Be careful though, and immediately remove any epoxy that runs out of the joint with acetone, otherwise, I'm afraid, your varnish will be completely ruined.

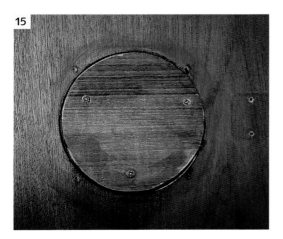

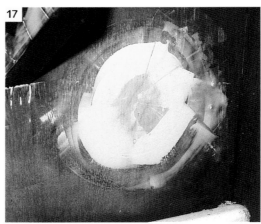

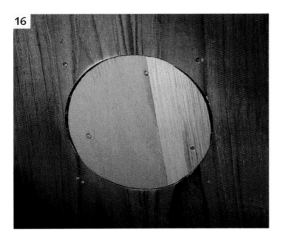

15 This bulkhead once carried a loudspeaker. This will now be removed so the remaining hole can be sealed. It's a fairly straightforward job. You merely glue a piece of wood across the hole from behind with epoxy resin. Once that's cured, you then insert a round piece of wood into the hole from the front and glue it into place.

16 The wooden plug should either be exactly the same thickness as the bulkhead or perhaps about 1mm thicker. If it's at all thinner, then you'll have to fill the entire area with filler which is far less satisfactory and will never look as good. Finally, sand down the wood so the edges are smooth with the bulkhead.

17 Check to see if the filler and the paint you want to use are compatible with each other. To find out, consult the manufacturer's instructions. As a general rule, you can always apply one-pot or two-pot paint on two-component filler – but, as I say, look at the relevant literature and consult your supplier if necessary.

18 You can, of course, always smooth out any of the smaller cracks with the filler, but remember you should never apply it too generously. Otherwise you'll have a lot of extra sanding to do which can be arduous and extremely time-consuming.

19 The original companionway boards were in two pieces and beyond repair. The veneer had come off and the edges were severely damaged. A new, one-piece board has been made from marine grade plywood. As you can see, we fitted a massive frame, then lightly sanded the wood, stained it with dark wood stain and applied four coats of clear varnish on top.

20 The holding battens along the sides of the hatch-board opening are made from stainless steel. The new board itself should slide in and out easily without much effort, so take extra care to make sure it's not too tight. Otherwise it might jam after varnishing.

21 All the covering battens should be cut slightly longer so that you have a bit in reserve for the final fit. They can then be sanded and varnished in the workshop before you fix them in position. If the inside of the hull is covered, you can leave small gaps between the battens which will improve the air flow and the general ventilation of the hull.

22 All the mahogany components have been varnished and finished off in the workshop, then packed in protective plastic and numbered to show where they go. This might sound like a lot of extra work, but it's much better than cutting, sanding and varnishing them in a small cabin on board.

23 Old teak oil can simply be washed out using thinners or acetone. Having said that, do make absolutely sure that the cabin is well ventilated while you're doing this – it's nasty stuff! The cleaned surfaces can then be sanded, which will have to be done by hand. I suggest you use only good quality 80 to 240 Grade paper.

24 Joints that take a lot of strain can be glued together using thickened epoxy resin. Small uneven gaps can also be filled with a thick epoxy mixture. For simple jobs, it's a good idea to make the mix slightly thinner. You can also adjust the pot life of the epoxy by using different hardeners.

25 While the epoxy cures, the battens are held in place by screw cramps. As an extra precaution you should always insert small strips of hardwood between the cramps and the batten to protect the varnish. Be careful not to tighten the screw cramps too much, because they will otherwise leave small dents in the battens.

26 If larger plywood panels are to be glued to each other as is the case here, where we're preparing the sides for a new hanging locker in the saloon, screw cramps alone might not be enough. To hold the panels in place while the epoxy cures, therefore, also use battens which should be wedged into place.

Improving the appearance below

How to make your saloon look more attractive: instead of simple lids, use opening doors on lockers, add wooden trim, and work in some contrast to liven everything up.

Wood is the most traditional boat building material, and still widely used, even in modern fibreglass construction, especially below decks. Teak, mahogany and other high quality hard woods often face-up otherwise bare plastic hulls on the inside, to inject character and provide a feeling of warmth, as well as insulating against moisture, heat, cold and noise. In other words, just about every yacht will have a certain amount of woodwork on board.

1 Wood replacing plastic. The formerly naked fibreglass cabin side now disappears behind a six-millimetre plywood panel with an attractive, even grain.

2 This is how the experts do it. Corners are smoothed and rounded with a sanding machine.

3 The original interior of the boat. As you can see, dark cabin sides and upholstery gives the small saloon an even smaller feel; similarly, oiled teak deteriorates over the years – and too many screw heads and other bits and pieces spoil the appearance of the wooden bulkheads and deckhead.

4 The full extent of the damage becomes evident after all the fittings have been removed. The only answer in a case like this is a complete refit. It would also make sense to choose a light coloured paint to give a brighter feel.

5 These locker doors are a good example of how the whole of the interior should look when it's all finally completed. White panels are surrounded by chunky mahogany frames. High gloss white paint adds a dramatic contrast and also highlights the effect of the wood. The saloon looks roomier too.

Using the example of our old Avance 24, we want to show you how the appearance and the feel of the interior can be improved by using new cladding and fitting different doors etc. It may look quite daunting but, in fact, assuming you use the proper tools and techniques, it's relatively easy to make all the items shown here – so you can do it yourself. To make it all less stressful, of course, many of the preparatory steps like cutting, sanding and varnishing can be done in the comfort of your garage, shed or workshop at home. As before, you'll need some basic equipment and a reasonable assortment of tools, including a proper workbench, mitre jig, several drills,

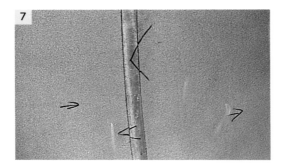

grindstone, various chisels, sanding machines, and a heavy-duty vacuum cleaner – not to mention a generous supply of sand or glass paper in various grades, paint remover, varnish and thinners, fibreglass mats and epoxy resin, plus a set of screw cramps.

The next question is deciding the most suitable type of wood. Mahogany, for example, is easy to work with, easy to bond and looks good when varnished. Teak, on the other hand, is oilier, more expensive and significantly more difficult to bond properly. Which ever kind of timber you eventually

6 These plain, bare fibreglass sides in the forepeak of our boat will be covered with strips of wood. First, vertical mounting strips are fastened to the sides. If the hull is a sandwich laminate, they can simply be screwed on; but if it's solid, each one will have to be glued in place instead. Saw cuts in the back of the strips help make them more flexible so you can bend them to shape the contour of the hull.

7 Having cut the panels to size you then need to check them to make sure they fit perfectly. The next step is to mark them with a felt-tip pen so that they can then be glued into place.

8 With the first stage complete, you can now fit the covering battens. Use several power drills and screwdrivers so you don't have to constantly change the bits etc in the drill head. You'll need a small drill for the screws, a slightly larger diameter drill for the through-holes in the battens, and a 90-degree countersink for the screw heads.

9 Use a provisional and flexible batten to determine the exact lengths of the covering strips. Cut the strips the length with a jigsaw but be careful not to damage the front surface by cutting from behind. Long strips need a two to four millimetres gap at each end for thermal expansion.

choose, however, it's best to buy all of it, including the battens from a proper yachting source such as a boatyard or specialised wood supplier rather than using several different outlets. That's because you want to make sure that they can either readily supply the often unusual shapes and profiles found in a yacht's interior, or cut them to order.

But how much wood is really necessary? After all, your boat already has a finished interior so you're not exactly starting from scratch. Obviously, to a great extent, the answer depends on your individual needs and

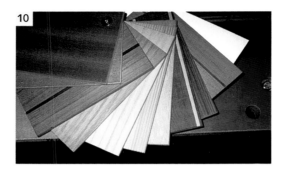

10 Solid wood and plywood. There are many types of wood besides teak and mahogany you could use but not all of them are suitable for boat-building. Nordic softwoods are less suitable for a boat interior because they tend to be too soft. Cherry and maple, on the other hand, are extremely good alternatives.

11 If you want to change 90-degree corners to 45-degree seams, you'll need a mitre jig. Before cutting the wood, make a few test cuts in some scrap pieces to align the jig. The cuts must be exact; otherwise you'll have gaps in the seams.

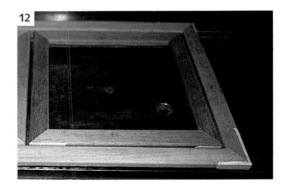

12 After the strips have been cut to size, they can be glued together with epoxy. But before you start, you should first place all the parts together to check for a proper fit. When gluing, you don't need a great deal of epoxy to achieve a solid bond. Small gaps can always be filled with epoxy that has been thickened to a suitable consistency.

13 When the frames have been bonded and cured, you can work out exactly where you want to put the hinges. Place them in the appropriate position on the frames, and mark round them with a soft pencil or felt-tip, then cut away a small amount of the wood using a wood-chisel, and finally screw them firmly into place.

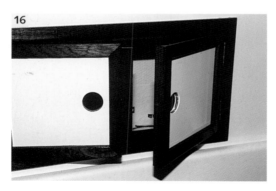

desires. For example, if you want to replace simple or perhaps flimsy sliding hatches in the saloon lockers with solid opening doors, you'll need wooden door fronts and battens. To clad the interior of a fibreglass hull, or improve the look of your bulkheads, you can use plywood panels or lining battens. And again, different colours and contrasts can greatly enhance a yacht's interior appearance. So it's a question of how far you want to go. As far as the overall appearance is concerned, as a general rule on small yachts, large or flat areas should be kept as light as possible, while frames and other timber trim can be made of a darker wood to provide an attractive contrast.

14 There are all sorts of different possibilities for door locks. We chose the conventional type because they work well and are really easy to mount. Small, stainless steel hooking plates were screwed on the back of each of the left-hand side doors.

15 On each of the right hand doors we fitted small catches which can be accessed through these round finger-holes. But one simple reminder: you should always fix catches like these in such a way that you can operate them with your right hand, otherwise it can be extremely awkward.

16 This is how the doors work in practice; it's all perfectly straightforward. You merely close the left hand half and push the hooking pin down to secure it. The right hand door then closes against a part of the left-hand frame. The catch should now fit without having to exert any undue pressure.

17 The newly designed sides of the saloon. As you can see, the door frames and the wood around the window have been stained dark, then varnished four times. The white panels have been painted with several coats of a high gloss white paint to lighten everything up.

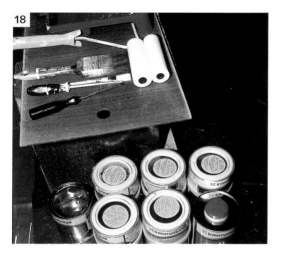

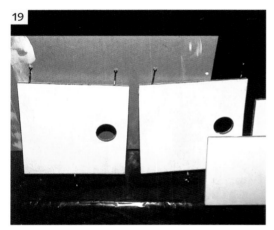

18 You need a clean workplace when working with varnishes, paints, thinners and brushes. You should also try to keep the environment as free of dust as possible. Seal all your tins and containers with cling film or something similar - because dust is your worst enemy, whatever coating you use.

19 It makes sense and saves a great deal of time if you paint both sides of each door in one go. To go about it you simply screw four long wood screws into the sides of the timber and use them as temporary handles. What could be simpler.

20 Hanging it all out to dry. Thin, plastic lines like these can be used to support the still wet, freshly varnished strips of wood and, apart from anything else, saves time. Don't worry about the tiny marks they leave; just ignore them. They won't show once the varnish has finally dried.

21 Before these long, thin covering strips have been varnished, you should sand them down and clean them thoroughly; as before, it's also a good idea to prepare a suitable area for stowing them whilst they dry. Again, you can use thin lines, tubes or hose to support them.

Renovating the galley

This galley module slides out into position in the saloon. With its polished steel, and contrasting timber it looks smart and practical – but needed an overhaul.

However small, every cabin should always find room for a cooker; it's an essential piece of equipment. After all, what cruising sailor wants to miss his cup of tea or coffee, or do without a tasty hot meal? Even our modest, 24-foot Avance has one. It's a simple, sliding model, based on a clever idea which first saw the light of day some thirty years ago. This particular version consists of a stove and sink, and is mounted on metal tracks. To get at it, you slide it out from the quarter berth, where

it also stows away when you're not using it. The module should slide easily as long as you keep the tracks and plastic sliders well lubricated with Teflon spray. You should also make sure that the fresh water and sink drain hoses don't get entangled, and fall neatly into position when you pull the unit out. Incidentally, as a safety precaution this cooker can be firmly locked in either position to keep it secure even in heavy seas.

When we bought the boat, the original sliding galley, which was already nearly a quarter of a century old, was still in near original condition. However, time had left its scars. It consisted of a paraffin cooker, a plastic sink and two drawers. The box itself was made of dark varnished plywood and the

1 Making the final adjustments to our new galley. The box, made from 16 millimetre plywood, was re-used, the cooker thoroughly overhauled and the sink replaced.

2/3 Before and after. The original unit was dark and dull and definitely needed cheering up. Now everything looks bright and more attractive.

surface was rough and uneven.

As it happened, we wanted to keep the paraffin cooker, partly because the fuel is readily available and partly because, with gas cookers we always worry about leaks. Paraffin for cookers can be obtained all over the world. And in cold weather, you can transform your cooker into a makeshift heater by simply placing a flower-pot over the flame. It's also difficult to fit a proper gas installation on a small boat, especially if you have a sliding galley like this one. It would have been necessary to fit a long, flexible gas hose which might not meet the necessary safety or legal regulations.

This particular make of paraffin cooker is still made today so spare parts are readily available, and overhauling it presented no real problems. But, in contrast, the old plastic sink was beyond repair. The gelcoat was not only rough but also damaged in many places. A steel sink is a more practical proposition; it looks nicer, too. We also wanted to install a pivoting tap, which, given the thin sides of the fibreglass sink, would have been particularly difficult. Finally, the original galley had only one flexible water hose and a tap in the locker.

We also changed the appearance of the galley box to make it blend in better with rest of the new interior decor. This meant painting it a lighter colour, leaving contrasting dark mahogany trim around the edges.

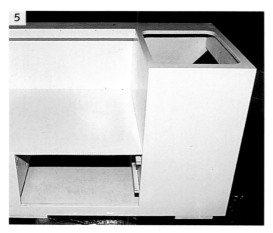

4 The procedure for sanding was much the same as it was for the rest of the interior. We took everything apart, thoroughly cleaned all the timber parts with acetone, then sanded them down. If you're fitting a new and perhaps different sized sink then the whole unit may need a new top.

5 Galleys are functional areas so, since the wooden surfaces will come in for a lot of hard use later on, the paint you use here must be particularly durable and tough – which is why we suggest a two-pot paint. It's always advisable to apply two or three coats to the surfaces.

6 The drawers were made from plastic and were quite robust, so we simply gave them a thorough clean. The larger surfaces can always be polished with a power tool, but the smaller areas and corners must be finished off by hand. If you find any scratches you can first treat them with sanding paste and then polish them out.

7 Originally, the drawers had what we thought were rather unattractive frames made from black plastic. To improve the appearance, we replaced them with chunky mahogany – the same wood we used throughout the rest of the boat. When staining the wood before varnishing, it's always advisable to try a test sample first.

8 As you can see, the drawers have finger holes just like the lockers. To finish them off we fitted pre-fabricated wooden rings of a kind which are normally made in the Far East. The precise measurements can often vary slightly, so it's vital that you try them for size and, if necessary, sand them down to make them fit before varnishing.

9 The original galley only had a 'flying' or remote water hose with a small tap on the end which could be taken from the locker above. It worked well enough, but we felt that a much better solution would be a folding tap – which meant you could still slide the pantry back into the quarter berth.

10 We drilled a ten millimetre hole in the side of the new sink. It's not at all difficult but if you're doing a job like this make sure that you have a steady work surface. Using a round file, the hole was gently enlarged and then finally finished to the exact diameter. After that, we fitted the tap and the two gaskets in the hole.

11 Here you can see the actual drain of the sink, on which the flexible drain hose will be mounted – and which could be cut to size with a hacksaw. To make fastening of the drain easier, it makes sense to cover the threads with a thin film of acid-free lubricating grease.

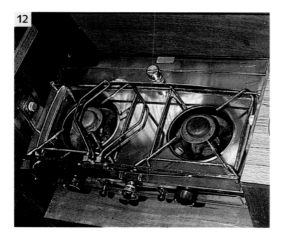

12 This original Swedish Optimus stove is still undoubtedly worth saving, even after so many years of use. Not only that, it's still sold today, to nearly the same specification. Spare parts are readily available too, and it's relatively easy to take apart without specialist knowledge. That's why so many skippers like them; some even prefer them to gas.

13 Stoves which are well maintained seldom cause problems. However, blockages can and do occur. The double pipes for the pre-heating system are particularly vulnerable, but in the final analysis, if all else fails, it's possible to close them off and pre-heat the stove with white spirit.

14 The pre-heating tablet underneath the burner gets dark and discoloured over the years. Part of the problem is the fact that burnt food also collects here. So, what can you do about it? Well, the kind of steel brush used for pots and pans will help to clean it again. But take it easy and don't ever scrub too enthusiastically, otherwise you could cause more damage and the surface could rust later on.

15 Almost as good as new. After a thorough overhaul, our stove has been fully restored and is in virtually pristine condition. The left-hand burner was replaced completely, because the underside had been damaged by the pre-heating system.

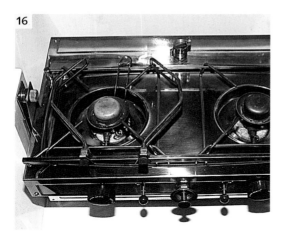

16 When cooking at sea, it's absolutely vital that the stove can swing up to 40 degrees on either side. Surprisingly though, even cookers on newly built yachts don't always meet this important requirement. So take care not to fit the fixing points for the swinging axis either too low or too far back.

17 These adjusting screws control the friction and determine how easily the stove can swing at sea. By tightening them up, two leather gaskets are pressed together – which dampens the swing. If these discs are missing or seem hard and brittle, replace them. These screws also enable you to lock the stove securely when in harbour.

18 This massive plywood top has more than one use, and doubles as a chart table, so must be strong enough to cope with someone leaning on it. The hinges have to be strong too and are made of heavy-duty stainless steel. The same goes for the screws, which should also be stainless steel and at least 30 millimetres long.

19 Finally, don't forget to test the stove. Even if you're confident about your work, always have a fire extinguisher handy just in case one of the pipes should leak. After the pre-heating phase, a steady, blue flame should be burning. Always keep a careful eye on the pressure gauge which should read between 1 and 1.5 bar.

Insulation and interior linings

Most boat interiors use three basic materials: wood, fibreglass and what I call flexible synthetics. In this chapter we take a look at how such materials are often used in boat building, how proper insulation can create a comfortable interior environment, and how to avoid condensation.

Many boat owners extend their season from early spring well into late autumn. That's when the differences between inside and outside temperatures are most pronounced, and people tend to spend more nights on

1 Using a sharp pair of scissors and a knife, most imitation leather fabrics can easily be cut to size. Leave around five to eight millimetres extra around the edges so you can fix them.

board, perhaps using the boat like a holiday home. The problem however is that fibreglass is a relatively poor insulator. It may be slightly better than steel or aluminium, but it's certainly not as good as wood. So if the boat isn't properly insulated, you'll find condensation forming, which, in turn, encourages bacteria and mildew – not to mention that nasty, mouldy old smell which inhabits so many boats which are getting on a bit.

So, what actually happens? Well, condensation occurs down below when warm air which has a high humidity content comes into contact with the cold sides of the boat. Because the air cools down, it can't hold on to the humidity any longer, which in turn, forms small drops of condensation. After a while, a thin film of moisture covers the inside of the hull. To make matters worse, if the boat's ventilation is bad, and you make the mistake of using the gas cooker to warm you up (which produces even more humidity) you'll produce a very damp environment indeed.

The aim therefore is to reduce the risk of condensation as much as possible. The best insulation barrier, of course, is a vacuum; the second best is air. It goes without saying that a vacuum is completely impractical, but we can certainly make use of air – either in the usual, traditional way by simply leaving a gap between the wooden interior cladding and the sides of the hull – or by using a form of foam cladding. Closed cell foams contain 97 per cent air, have very good insulation characteristics and don't burn. That's why, in my view you should use it to cover the whole of the hull on the inside down below. As an additional bonus, some products like foam-backed, simulated leather serve two purposes at once. With five-millimetres of insulating foam already permanently glued on the back, they not only provide insulation but also look good as well.

However, humidity can also condense under the berths, assuming the mattress lies directly on the colder base beneath. Again, to stop that happening, you should add an insulating layer of air. You can easily do that with the help of an insulating webbing material which should be placed between the mattress and the berth itself. The picture sequence here shows various different kinds of insulating material, and explains how you can make use of it on your boat.

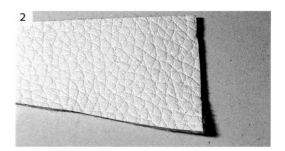

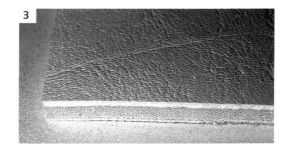

2 Synthetic fabrics with webbing on one side are not only easy to use, but also washable and come in different colours. The material stretches and is suitable for smooth surfaces but has no real insulating qualities.

3 Imitation, or simulated leather and foam provide insulation and can also greatly improve a boat's appearance. This particular kind of material also hides any bumps or unevenness in the laminate and prevents condensation.

4 Insulating foam like this is simple to work with and can easily be stuck on with contact glue. The covering foil stops the adhesive from penetrating the foam.

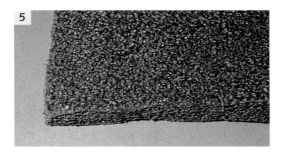

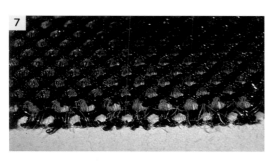

5 Foam without any covering film on the top can be glued to large surfaces with special glue specifically designed for the job. The foam itself is a particularly good insulator and can be covered with a decorative surface fabric.

6 There are numerous insulating materials you can use; Dryweave is a polyester 3-D fabric that stops condensation between the berth and the mattress. It consists of 95 percent air and is reasonably strong.

7 Here's another example: Thermo-Flex is a 3-D insulating fabric that slides in between the mattress and the sheet. This again also holds back condensation.

8 Dry-d-Tex is an open lining fabric and is another example of the sort of material you could use. The back is covered with a closed fabric that's fairly easy to glue. It provides good ventilation and can also be used successfully to reduce noise in the cabin.

9 This smart leatherette material has an insulating foam core and a textured back that bonds very well with the glue.

10 A staple gun like this is absolutely essential if you're covering boards with fabric. Once the fabric has been stretched in place, it can be held with six millimetre stainless steel staples.

11 Choose a glue that's solvent free but don't mix it with thinners. Thinners, however, can be used to remove any remains of old glue. Apply it to one side only; leave to ventilate, and simply slide the covering layer in place.

12 You can make a clean cut with a sharp pair of scissors or a knife. Long edges must be marked with a felt-tip pen using a long steel ruler.

13 Roller or brush? Use a brush for tight corners and smaller areas, while applying glue to large areas with a felt or foam roller. The layer of glue will be thinner when you use a foam roller. But only use the roller once.

14 You'll find that yachts which date from the 1960s and 1970s are often fitted with a synthetic sort of foil down below. The material itself is OK, but the surface becomes dull and dirty over time. The other problem is that mildew often forms behind it too. For those reasons, I suggest you remove all of it during the refit and start again.

15 Depending on the particular glue they used, removing the foil can either be extremely easy or very difficult. If it sticks to the sides like it did on our boat, you can only shave it off with a sharp knife or metal spatula. The fibreglass surface should then be cleaned with thinners and finally sanded.

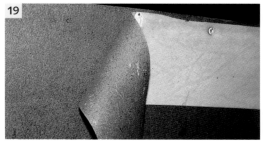

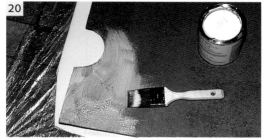

16 Rather than covering the hull sides with fabric again, we opted for wooden cladding made of mahogany strips. As a base, we glued vertical strips of wood to the hull every 60 to 80 centimetres. We then filled the space in between by gluing foam to the hull.

17 I recommend you choose a glue that's solvent free and, for that reason, doesn't smell. Buy one that's easy to apply with either roller or brush. After the glue has been applied and left to breathe according to the instructions, it should only need slight pressure to achieve a really good bond.

18 Insulating foam glued to the hull. You should expect to use about 200 to 400 grammes of glue for one square metre. Gluing usually takes between about 20 and 40 minutes. After allowing the glue to breathe, just press lightly into place.

19 This is how you remove the old foil. Simply cut the material into narrow strips with a knife, then just tear it off. This is easier and more efficient than trying to pull it off in large chunks.

20 Apply the glue with a roller where ever possible. The film you leave behind will then be much more even. I suggest you only use a brush for the smaller areas.

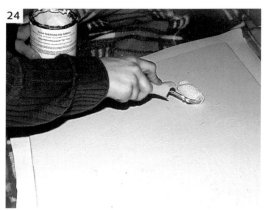

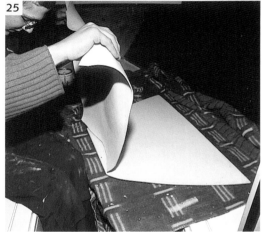

21 Cut the leatherette into a star shape, stretch it in place, and fix it immediately with staples because the glue alone won't hold it in place right away.

22 Covering a section in the anchor locker. First make a six-millimetre strong plywood panel. Leave about two millimetres around the sides to make sure it still fits after you've added the leatherette. Then cut the imitation leather, adding five millimetres around the edges.

23 It makes sense to apply the glue you choose with a small roller, but not, of course, before all the pieces of material have been cut to the right size.

24 Spread the glue while it's still white. Once it begins to go off, don't try to spread it any more. The finger-test will tell you when it's time to stick the prepared fabric in position. Touch lightly with your finger and remove. If the material clings to your skin, you can start putting it on!

25 Before fitting the lining always clean your hands with thinners. Hold the fabric along the upper edge and then push the lower edge into place. Only apply light pressure, then carefully ease the material into position.

26 Spread the lining from the middle, working from the centre out towards the edges until all the air bubbles have disappeared. If necessary, you might have to lift the material off a little, then stick it back on again. This usually works as long as the glue hasn't gone off too much.

27 Now's the time to start covering the back edges of the board with glue, again, waiting until it starts to react before you go any further.

28 Wrap the long edges of the foil around the plywood board, applying light pressure, before fixing with stainless staples. This job is a whole lot easier with two people - one wrapping the lining around and holding it in place, while the other fixes it with the staples, using one every ten millimetres or so.

29 After drilling all the necessary holes, the finished board must then be screwed securely in place. Surface washers should be used to stop the leatherette from wrapping itself around the screw-heads when you drive them in.

Servicing fittings and deck gear

Fairlead or winch, stanchion or traveller, hatch, cleat or ventilator – after your refit, everything you take off and refurbish should last for another 25 years.

1 Finishing touches on deck. This polished pulpit looks as if it just came out of the box. When we fitted it, each bolt was carefully sealed.

At last, both the hull and the deck of our boat are almost back to their original condition; the weeks of sanding, fairing and painting are finally over, and we can move on to the next stage. Now it is time to take a close look at the boat's gear and equipment and decide what to do with it.

All the fittings we removed in the autumn, at the start of our refit, must now be taken apart, overhauled and put back together again. Only when everything is functioning perfectly again will each component be allowed back to its old (sometimes new) home on deck. Fittings which are too far gone and beyond repair, or which are simply out of date by today's standards, should, of course, be replaced.

Inevitably, the work-list will be a long one, particularly if you want to reorganise the way you do things. In our case, the old, non self-tailing genoa winches, for example, will be overhauled, then mounted on the coachroof to act as winches for the halyards and trimming-lines – replacing a tiny winch that, with luck, will probably be sold at the next boat jumble. In front of each winch we shall fit a row of stoppers to provide flexibility. Previously, a colourful assortment of different sized cleats and jammers was scattered around this particular area, but the new arrangement will allow us to operate eight lines from the cockpit.

The old hatch on the foredeck will also have to be replaced. It was too dilapidated to be saved but, luckily, we found a brand new model which exactly fitted the old dimensions.

Other new items included two designer cleats made by Nomen and a traveller. The old track was scruffy, the wheels of the car sticky, and a fine-adjustment pulley was missing altogether.

In contrast, all the stainless steel parts, like the pulpit and pushpit, stanchions and ventilators, were polished and refurbished. The sliding hatch over the companionway, made from acrylic glass, was buffed up with sanding paste. A light alloy frame protected the edges but we renewed the sliding strips, as the old ones were too short. We employed the services of a professional to clean, repolish and, where necessary, reanodise the alloy parts like cleats and handrails, to chromium plate brass hinges, and to regalvanise the anchor chain and the anchor itself. If you plan to follow suit, remember, it pays to get quotes from various companies. The procedures took a few days but after that, everything looked factory-fresh – and it was far cheaper than buying new.

2 As a matter of course, about every five years, winches should be taken apart, washed and then properly greased with the recommended lubricant. First, carefully prise off the spring clip with a screwdriver. The end of the ring has a small indent to make the job easier. If it's the first time you've done this, make a note of the way it all goes together.

3 To be able to reach the lower parts and the gears, you might have to take off the plinth. It's also essential if you plan to paint the deck underneath. But make it easy on yourself. Cleaning and re-assembling the winch is much easier in your garage or workshop at home.

4 A glance inside tells you everything you need to know. Clearly, this particular winch hasn't been greased very often over the years. A sure sign of neglect is the fact that the grease itself is sticky and full of metal particles. This accelerates wear and greatly reduces the efficiency of the winch. It's obviously time for a refit.

5 This is how you get to the gears. First put a handle into the winch and fix it head down in a vice. Now you have to remove the screw on the underside of the winch. If it's stuck, take the biggest possible screwdriver you can find and loosen the screw by banging it with a hammer.

6 The mechanism can now be removed fairly easily. You should always take special care that you don't lose any of the tiny springs etc which can easily fall out and disappear. It always helps to spread an old sheet or bedspread underneath the vice to catch anything that might drop out accidentally.

7 As you can probably see, this particular lower bearing clearly shows a lack of maintenance; it's not been greased for many a long year. Luckily, things aren't too bad and it can still be used. However, as a general rule, if the rollers of the bearing are damaged or distorted too much, you might have to replace them.

8 This inner gear rim shows fewer signs of deterioration; that's because the forces here are somewhat less than those actually inside the gears. The pinion has to turn several times while the outer casing turns only once. For that reason, you rarely have to replace the outer casing.

9 The inner drive shaft with the two pawls has been dismantled. You should clean both sets of ratchet braces, and check the spring clips as well as the edges. If the latter are damaged, exchange the whole lot. That way you avoid any risk that the winch might suddenly kick back when you use it – which could be extremely dangerous at sea.

10 Every winch has two sets of pawls or ratchet braces; one up on the drive shaft, the other, a lower pair, on the casing. Once pushed in position, small steel spring clips hold them in place. If the grease is sticky, it's possible that the pawls won't grip so the winch will no longer work properly. Instead it will simply spin round when you use it to tighten a sheet or halyard.

11 Rain or salt water will quickly wash away the grease along the drive shaft. This particular component is exposed more than any other part of the winch and if the teeth are dented or damaged, the shaft will have to be replaced. Always use waterproof grease!

12 After dismantling the winch you need to leave all the parts to soak in paraffin for about 30 minutes. Then clean thoroughly with a brush. Finally, rinse in fresh paraffin, and make sure everything's dry. If the paraffin fails to remove all the dirt and stains, try soaking and rinsing in a second bath of thinners.

13 Once you've removed all the old grease and dirt from every one of the components, cover everything generously with new winch grease. Finally, put the winch back together and make sure it works properly. It should now turn extremely easily without any problems at all. You should also hear a regular clicking noise.

14 Over the years, the zinc layer on this chain has worn rather thin. Given the hard life it's led, that's hardly surprising. Anyhow, because of that, rust has already developed in some places. To get back to bare metal, the remaining zinc will be stripped off in a bath of hydrochloric acid. The whole process only takes a few minutes.

15 As you can see, after our highly effective acid treatment, the old zinc layer has almost vanished completely, revealing further corrosion. Further immersion in the stripping bath won't remove it, so something more abrasive is called for. Sandblasting is the obvious answer at this stage.

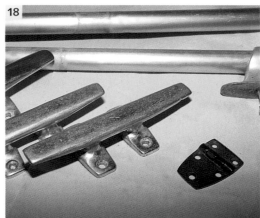

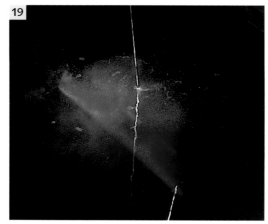

16 The chain has to go back into the acid once more to remove all traces of zinc, paint and dirt. This is because the surface must be chemically clean before the new galvanising process can be applied. The final stage of the treatment takes place in an ultrasonic tank.

17 Our newly galvanised chain emerges. The zinc layer looks incredibly bright and shiny but, for all that, is still rather thin. If you want an even thicker coating, because your particular chain gets a lot of regular use on a winch perhaps, then this may be unsuitable and you should really opt for spray galvanising instead.

18 The original alloy cleats, fittings and hand-holds that came off the boat were really quite scruffy. Even so, they can still be refurbished because the basic material is still sound. Even the dull brass hinge can be polished or chrome plated.

19 First, you have to remove the old anodising layer in a special bath. Once immersed, the alloy parts will start to foam until the layer has been completely removed; this is the initial stripping process. In practice, it takes only a few minutes but completely removes the old layer from the fittings.

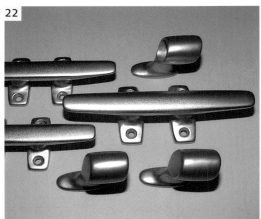

20 After the stripping stage has been completed, the fittings have to be sanded down to make good any mechanical damage. This kind of work requires a high degree of sensitivity, as well as care and control, otherwise the process can easily produce new scratches and actually make things worse instead of better.

21 The next step, after all this, is the fine polishing. The anodising layer is, in fact, so thin that it doesn't hide any scratches left after sanding. The better the polish, the better the overall result. All the surfaces should be polished until every single scratch has disappeared leaving a bright, even surface.

22 Just about as good as new again. After polishing, the fittings have to be cleaned once more in a chemical bath, then finally anodised. The result is a new and fairly strong surface. These days, it's even possible to have your fittings anodised in various different colours such as blue, red or black. It's up to you.

23 We even decided to refurbish the anchor. As you can probably see, the right fluke has already been treated by blasting with ceramic powder which removes all signs of corrosion and dirt before the final process takes place. Even larger items can easily be treated using the same method.

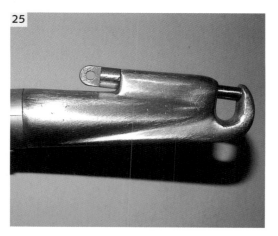

24 The end fitting on the spinnaker-pole has been badly damaged over the years. It has become dented and scratched. What's the answer? Well, you could always use a nylon brush to partly restore the appearance but remember, if you do this it will inevitably produce a rather dull surface.

25 You could also polish this end fitting if you wanted to. In fact, though, it's hardly worthwhile because it will quickly get scratched again when you use it at sea. If you really insist on making this item look as good as new, there's only one course of action: you must take it apart and have it reanodised by a specialist.

26 Our extremely stylish designer cleat by Nomen has been dismantled prior to fitting. No special tools are required for this kind of job which is easy and straightforward. Simply remove the bolts and the two arms, as well as the rubber ball to expose the ground plate. This can then be fitted to the deck with three stainless M8 bolts.

27 After that, you have to first drill some small holes to hold the fitting in place, then some 8.5 millimetre holes right through the deck. A word of warning however: when you're doing this, take special care that you hold the drill exactly vertically to ensure that the bolts will also be vertical.

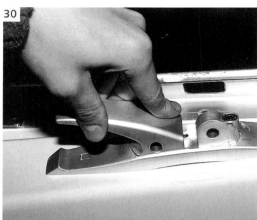

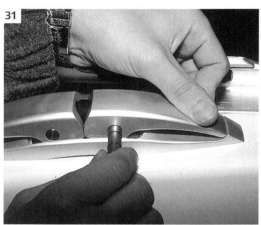

28 Alternatively, you could drill only one hole, then simply bolt the fitting to the deck and drill the other holes using the fitting as a template. There's a possible snag with this though. While you're drilling, take special care not to damage the edges of the holes in the base plate of the fitting. This could affect the fit or even allow gaps for moisture.

29 When all the holes have eventually been drilled you need to apply some sealant around their edges. But it's vital that you don't squeeze any sealant underneath the base plate itself. If you do, rainwater might easily get trapped inside the fitting and cause problems later.

30 Fitting the cleat. Insert and tighten all three bolts, using washers underneath the deck to provide grip. Take care that the base plate of the fitting sits evenly on the deck. If it doesn't, it probably means the holes weren't drilled exactly vertically. If that is what's happened, it might help if you very carefully make the holes slightly larger.

31 As you can probably see, assembling this particular kind of cleat is simplicity itself. This is the sequence: you merely insert one arm first, then slide the slightly greased bolt into place. Next, put the rubber ball into the joint, add the second arm and finally slide in the bolt.

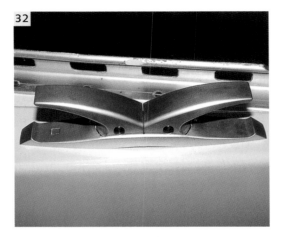

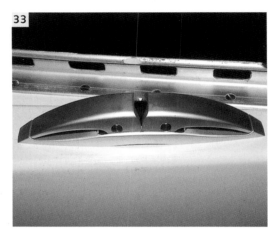

32 This cleat has been extremely well fitted. The base plate sits nice and evenly on the deck, while the small gap between the middle of the plate will allow rainwater to drain off freely without causing any trouble. You should now also check that the bolts are completely watertight by spraying some water over them.

33 At the end of all this, time for the final quality control. If the cleat has been mounted correctly, the horns should be able to move extremely easily. If not, the cleat might not have been fitted properly. The horns can be raised by lightly tapping the middle of the cleat.

34 The sealant used on the original hatch has been completely destroyed. Worse still, the hinges are sticky and the hatch itself is also leaking. Repairing something like this would be completely impractical if not ridiculously expensive. The only sensible answer is a new hatch.

35 Old silicone sealant can stick to the boat in such a way that it becomes a real problem to remove. If that's what's happened, you should lift the frame off with a screwdriver, bit by bit. Don't use brute force, but be patient and take it gently. If you take your time, the sealant will slowly respond to the pressure and gradually come unstuck.

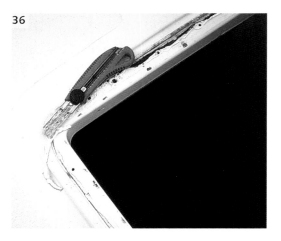

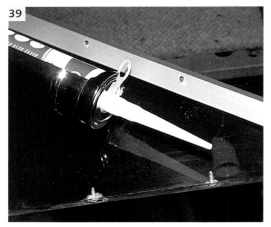

36 Cut the sealant with a strong sharp knife once the frame has been prised up. Tackle it piece by piece and don't use a knife with a narrow blade because it can easily break. Once the frame has been removed, you can simply scrape away the rest of the sealant with a chisel.

37 Very gently sand down the fibreglass surface so it's even and clean. Then check to make sure that the holes fit the new frame. Apply sealant to the frame and fit it in place. Next, insert the screws and tighten lightly. Only tighten the screws fully the next day when the sealant has had some time to cure. Cut away excess sealant with a sharp knife.

38 This acrylic sliding hatch is dull, not very transparent any more, and damaged along the edges. To get it back into shape, apply some sanding paste with a brush, then slowly polish the surface. Take care that the plastic doesn't get warm at all, otherwise you'll leave polish marks on the surface.

39 Two rectangular aluminium strips form the U-shaped cover along the damaged edges. Fix it in place with sealant and then tighten up the screws. If the hatch is simply too old and damaged, you should exchange it for a new one. When choosing a suitable replacement, remember, Lexan hatches are highly durable and strong.

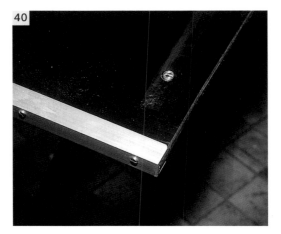

40 Remove the strip underneath the hatch. Then sand and treat it with three coats of paint. After the paint has completely dried, screw it back on again with a transparent sealant like Sikaflex. The hatch will not only look good again but also be transparent and let the light in once more.

41 The original sliding strips were too short. The new strips are made of stainless steel. The holes for the screws have been drilled with a special drill designed for stainless steel. Cool with cooling oil while drilling. Long shavings show that the drill is working properly. Smooth the holes after drilling, then polish the strips.

42 Here we have two new threaded terminals for our new wire guard rails. The first step is to provisionally fit the bottle-screw on the wire to see how much you need to cut off. Then you pull the wire tight, and hold the terminal in place. The mark in the thread cap shows precisely where you need to cut the wire.

43 Now you can cut the wire with a strong pair of bolt cutters. If you don't have any bolt cutters, the best thing to do is to cover the wire with tape and cut it with a hacksaw instead. The tape is important because it holds all the wire strands in place. If you don't use it you won't be able to fit the terminal afterwards.

44

46

45

47

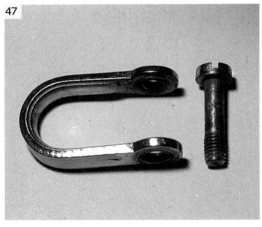

44 One terminal consists of three pieces. The inner wedged cap goes over the seven inner strands of the wire, while twelve strands remain outside. Push the wedged cap on to the wire until the outer strands are a millimetre longer. If the ends of these protruding strands aren't completely even, you should trim them now.

45 First push the outer thread cap over the wire, then add the eye terminal and screw in tightly. Open once more and check the position of the wire strands. All the ends of the wire must be bent backwards. They should never sit one above the other. Finally screw everything back together tightly and fit the guard rail wire.

46 For brightening up metal components, you'll need a power sander, rough and fine grade discs, and a 450-watt drill – along with a polishing disc, several nylon discs and a polishing head for the drill. For the final touch, you might try using stainless steel scourers. The sort used for cleaning pots can be particularly useful.

47 Even shackles made from stainless steel can develop rust on the surface. However that won't normally weaken the material. The whole effect is purely cosmetic and not normally a cause for concern. You can easily remove surface rust with a nylon brush. But wear gloves and protective goggles when you're doing it.

48 The rust in this thread was there when it left the manufacturer. That's because the hardened steel tool with which the thread was cut inevitably leaves small particles of steel behind that eventually rust. It won't actually weaken the material. Removing the rust simply improves the appearance.

49 This is how good the thread can look again even after many years. Clean with the nylon brush, then polish with the polishing head of the drill. Lightly oiled, with luck this will stay clean for at least the next 25 years!

50 Rubberised, self-amalgamating tape is a fantastic invention which has a huge number of uses on board. It can be stretched and twisted and will still act as a good sealant for small holes. Your fingers will stay clean and the tape will stay in place as if by magic. It's available at all good chandlers.

51 This kind of tape is wonderful to work with and can be rolled off and easily torn by hand without using a knife. If you want to make a round seal for example, you should first stretch the tape carefully, then tear it off and roll it into a round shape.

52 This home-made ring was placed in position after the surface was first thoroughly cleaned. Take particular care that the ring doesn't obstruct the hole for the screw, otherwise it might get damaged when you actually insert the screw itself.

53 The electrical wire for this lamp is exposed where it comes out of the hole, and could easily chafe, which could be extremely dangerous. Again, self-amalgamating rubberised tape could come in handy. Make a small ring and push it into the hole around the wire. This won't chafe any more and it's also protected.

THE WOODEN YACHT

Restoring a wooden yacht

This boat is about 20 years old and, as you might expect, is beginning to show her age. But if a wooden boat like this is still essentially sound, it can always be restored. Here's how to go about it.

Is it really worth restoring an old wooden yacht with your own bare hands? To be totally honest, the answer is probably no – at least not if you look at it in purely financial terms. If that's the most important consideration to you, I would probably advise you against it.

But many boat owners also actually enjoy working on their boats; they get pleasure from painting and varnishing and doing things their own way – they derive immense satisfaction from the whole idea of refitting and refurbishing – and using hands-on practical skills. For many, when they compare it with the kind of work they do for a living, it's a dramatic and welcome contrast. Among the majority of DIY enthusiasts, it's probably true to say that professional craftsmen are in a minority – many more have completely different jobs. But that's no real surprise. A bank manager will probably enjoy varnishing a teak hatch far more than studying accounts or working out exchange rates in his spare time.

So if you want to take on a restoration, I would suggest you only start working on an old boat if you plan to do it for your own satisfaction, and if you accept that the work involved is simply an enjoyable part of your hobby. Only if you take pride in your own craftsmanship, and get real satisfaction from it, will you feel adequately rewarded for your efforts. I can't make the point too strongly: never try and measure all the hard work in terms of saving money. And don't over-estimate your own practical abilities. Not everyone who can handle a jigsaw is also sufficiently qualified to fit a new teak deck. And many frustrated amateur boat builders have given up after weeks of hard labour, largely because they chose too big and complex a project in the first place. Worse still, if they then have to call in professional help from a boatyard to finish off the work, the bill will be enormous. On the other hand, there are many DIY boat builders around who happily and successfully restored their own boats. It's all a matter of judgement and common sense. To begin with, it's far better to choose a smallish boat which only needs cosmetic work to bring it back into shape.

1 At first sight, this popular family cruiser-racer didn't look too bad, but, in fact, after close examination we found plenty of work to do.

2 The first step when starting a project like this, is to take off all fittings. It's absolutely essential if you want to remove the paint and to treat the wood. But don't just throw them all into one big box; tape the screws to the fittings and mark them. Damaged fittings can be kept as a reference when you're choosing new ones.

3 This is a cast iron keel which has suffered from

a general lack of maintenance for many years. It's covered with a thick film of rust which has to be removed until you get down to the bare metal – then treated with a protective coating. Only after completing the basic treatment can the new antifouling be applied.

4 If layer after layer of paint have been added over the years, this is what you end up with. It's now time to remove all the old paint layers and get back to the bare wood, using various techniques such as scraping and stripping, hot air and sanding.

5 Removing the deck covering. This is a time-consuming task because you have to proceed gently, and with care. Remove each layer, one at a time.

6 The Waarschip 570 is an attractive little boat, examples of which can be found all over Europe. LOA 5.70 m; LWL 5.25 m; Beam 2.45 m; Draft 0.6 or 1 m; Displacement 0.8 tons; Ballast 0.3 tons; Berths 4; Construction: marine plywood.

It all starts with a new paint job. The paint industry today has products available which are not only easy for amateurs to use but which also produce near perfect results. For your first restoration project, the most sensible approach is to find a boat that's basically still sound. It could be one with a faded fibreglass hull, one built of plywood, or even one made of cold-moulded veneers. But steer well away from old, rusty steel boats, unless you're a metal boat expert. Similarly, don't buy a traditionally built wooden boat if it means replacing planks or frames. Big jobs like these require specialist knowledge, and a whole range of skills, and for that reason, are best left to the professionals.

Otherwise you might find yourself wasting a great deal of time and money on a project that, even after a huge amount of effort, could still, eventually fail.

By the same token, I would strongly urge you to avoid a wooden boat with a defective engine. Again, unless you're a really able and experienced mechanic, a big engine repair or rebuild can be tremendously expensive.

You should also try to pick a boat that's reasonably well known. Even if you do the restoration yourself, and plan to keep her – you never know; you might want to sell her some day. So before you get to that stage, it's worth remembering that popular, or well

7 This is what a window seal looks like after two decades. In its present state, it provides little protection, and water can seep inside virtually unhindered. To make matters worse, a moss-like substance growing between the wood and the window is slowly but surely destroying the timber which is now constantly moist.

8 Old varnish splits and cracks, especially when applied to solid timber, and provides an entry point. Moisture then gets into the wood, forming dark stains. You should treat such areas thoroughly, otherwise the wood will eventually be beyond repair. Remove all the varnish or paint immediately and leave the wood to dry.

9 This is how fittings come loose. Stanchions are especially vulnerable, particularly after so many years of use. Again, if you don't sort it out right away, water will find its way into the wood and begin a destructive process which might be hidden beneath a layer of paint until it's too late to do anything about it.

established models are easiest to sell. If there's an active class association, that's another important bonus. On the other hand, old boats of dubious ancestry are far harder to sell, unless, of course, you happen to find something of outstanding beauty, but, of course, such things are rare.

The example shown on these pages, is the Waarschip 500, a small wooden boat of a type you can see sailing all over European waters in their hundreds. She comes from a reputable yard and it's generally agreed that she also has a good sailing performance. She was built in the Netherlands and often sold in kit form, though complete or sailaway versions were available too. The plywood they used is of good marine quality but this particular boat was undoubtedly somewhat the worse for wear. Time had taken its toll. Overall though, this was an ideal project for us, because, while the boat had been clearly neglected, she was basically sound. Amateurs with average DIY skills and tools would be able to tackle all the necessary work without too much trouble.

We actually found the boat stored away in the far corner of a shed, and covered by a substantial layer of dust. If you're not an expert in wooden boats (yet), try and find someone who is – so they can help you check her over. Take a close look at the following

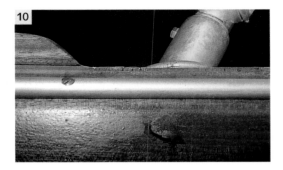

10 A screw incorrectly inserted can cause substantial damage. Here you can see how layers of wood have been forced apart by the screw. Because the varnish has also cracked, water has got into the wood. The only thing you can do here is to move the screw further inward and carefully seal this hole with a wooden plug.

11 Sharp corners with narrow seams open up a lot more easily. It's a common and notorious problem with all wooden boats. And even if you can hardly see the crack, water will get in and start the destructive process from the inside. Before getting to work, inspect the boat carefully for potential problems like this.

items and above all, take your time and make sure you have enough light. The bilge and the exposed ends of the keel-bolts; the keelson, the glued seams in the keel area, the bonding of the stringers, the rudder attachment, the area around the mast step – all need careful, close-up scrutiny. On the outside, carefully examine the hull-deck joint, the keel-hull joint, as well as the deck areas around fittings like stanchions, chainplates and cleats – not to mention the sliding hatch, the windows, the chainlocker and the forestay attachment.

Below decks, try and look into every nook and cranny. Warning lights should flash if you find any wet or soft spots in the timber. A well-maintained and well-built wooden boat should still be sound even after 20 years. Using a small screwdriver or even your fingernails, you can very easily find out if the wood is rotten or soft.

On the other hand, don't panic if the cast iron keel seems to have more rust than iron on the surface. You'll find enough sound metal left underneath – though it's a tedious and exhausting job stripping all the rust from the keel.

Having satisfied yourself that the hull, keel and rudder are sound, you can start to look at the rigging and equipment. Again, take your time and inspect everything closely. Unfortunately, owners of old boats who want to sell them will seldom tell you the whole truth.

Begin with the rigging and the fittings. A broken bottle-screw is easy and fairly cheap to replace but a damaged mast will be much more expensive. So how can you find out if it needs any work? Well, the mast profile should be free from dents or cracks. Look at the mast, particularly around the gooseneck fitting and crosstrees. Are there any sign of cracks here?

It's also possible that stainless steel screws or rivets have been used, in which case contact-corrosion could have weakened the aluminium profile of the mast. The usual tell-tale signs are white, salt-like flowering stains on the aluminium around the screws or rivets.

12 As you can see here, water has penetrated beneath the varnish causing discoloration. Rubbing strakes and similar parts on deck take a great deal of abuse so any varnish here will easily crack. And since more water will always get inside than can evaporate, the result, again, will be inevitable and slow degradation.

13 Time to relax and enjoy. When you can begin applying the new paint and varnish, you're starting the most pleasant part of the restoration. Up until then, you've been tediously taking things apart, sanding and preparing. The following chapters will show how you can achieve the final goal – without getting stressed.

As far as the sails are concerned, you might be lucky. After 20 years you can hardly expect them to be crisp and white but there's always a chance that the previous owner invested in a new suit of sails recently. If not, you might have to consider doing so yourself, in which case the price should be negotiated accordingly. But old sails can hardly be restored, so the alternative is to try and find good quality second-hand sails. Otherwise, the only other option is to simply buy some new ones.

This first chapter of the second part of this book was mainly aimed at giving you a few ideas and to whet your appetite. So now, if you really think you want to restore an old wooden boat, either for yourself or your children, you should start looking around for one. As well as all the usual places, try the less obvious as well – on beaches and foreshores for example. Then again, many basically sound boats may be hidden away in sheds and garages etc.

As to cost, prices for used boats in the

smaller range vary between maybe £2000 and £4000 ($3,345 and $6,690), depending on the amount of gear and equipment they come with. A road trailer and an outboard motor are of course extremely useful assets and well worth having. The 5.70 metre Waarschip used as an example here, was offered for sale with an asking price of £3,430 ($5,751). But remember, get hold of a sample contract for buying used boats. If you've not seen one before, contact the RYA for details. And one other thing, ask to see all the boat's papers and documents, including insurance certificates etc. That way, you can to some extent, make sure you're actually dealing with the rightful owner.

The following chapters will look at the restoration stages step-by-step. Repairing the cast iron keel, including the use of a chemical treatment; doing up the underwater hull; renewing the Perspex windows; installing a new forehatch; painting the hull with roller and brush; painting the deck; renewing and modifying the interior and repairing a delaminated wooden rudder.

Treating the keel

According to some people, cast iron keels start rusting in the brochure; in other words the problem is almost inevitable. Either way, the preventative measures described here should help keep it at bay.

Cast iron keels are cheap and easy to make; they also last a long time and aren't easily damaged – not even if the boat runs aground. The main drawback is that they rust. In most

1 Removing both the loose and the hard rust. Use a heavy-duty sander and a wire brush. Always wear protective goggles and a facemask.

cases, that won't really alter the stability of the boat, but it will affect her speed. The rough surface of a rusty keel acts like a brake. Ideally, then, the keel's surface should be as smooth as the rest of the underwater hull.

Every cast iron keel which has been bolted underneath the hull will inevitably start to

2

3

4

2 This is typical, good old fashioned rust. The iron itself has been changed by a process of oxidation. It turns red then crumbles away in tiny particles. To stop that happening, oxygen must be kept away from iron by using paint or other protective layers.

3 Light alloy doesn't rust in precisely the same way, but can still corrode, though it won't do so as quickly as iron. Still, any underwater components made of alloy should also be protected by the appropriate paint system.

Always fit sacrificial anodes to stop the alloy from being eaten away by electrolysis.

4 The joint between keel and hull is a notorious problem area and one where leaks can easily develop unless it's properly sealed. Never laminate over the seam, because the different characteristics of the materials mean they react differently to heat and cold, so you need a degree of flexibility. Always use silicone-free sealant that can be painted.

5 Once the bulk of the rust has been successfully removed, there's still work to do. Here we are, smoothing down the surface with an orbital sander. I would normally recommend 100 Grade sanding paper for this particular job.

6 Using a steel brush in the power drill is an excellent way of removing rough areas of rust and saves a great deal of time.

7 The edges must now be cleaned up with a chisel. Later on, you should get the boat lifted up in the crane so you can also clean the underside of the keel.

means removing all the rust and paint, getting back to the bare metal and applying a completely new protective paint system. The first part is a laborious and dirty job during which you should always wear protective goggles and a face mask. It's all far from pleasant but the rewards are enormous: if you do a thorough job, it means no more work on the keel for many years to come.

If, on the other hand, you only paint over the rust (and don't believe everything that some paint manufacturers would have you believe), you'll face exactly the same problem again and again, year after year. I'm afraid there's no quick-fix solution to this one.

When applying the paint, the first question people ask is: should I use a roller or a brush? The best answer, I think, is probably a combination of the two. It's best to use a foam roller for flat surfaces and a brush for all the corners and edges. And don't forget to throw away your rollers after each time you've used them; it's simply not worth the time and effort trying to wash them out. And anyway, you'll get far better results with a fresh roller than an old one with bits of paint stuck to it.

A keel which is simply bolted underneath the boat is usually easy to work on because all areas can be reached fairly easily – provided the boat has been propped up safely. You should

rust at some stage. The exceptions are those which have either been completely encapsulated in fibreglass – a good but expensive option – or those cast into the interior of the hull. The latter is less common these days because modern boats have more sophisticated underwater sections.

So let's assume we have a typical, run-of-the-mill boat, with a standard, bolted-on cast iron keel. Depending on the quality of the paint system, the first signs of rust will probably appear after about five years and soon spread over the entire keel. If that's the condition you find your boat in, nothing less than a thorough refit job will do, which

8 The roughly cleaned keel will always look a bit rust coloured if you use mechanical methods, because it's extremely difficult to remove every trace of corrosion from the small but sometimes fairly deep pores.

9 Using a rust-killer, applied methodically with a brush, you should be able to remove the very last particles of corrosion. After some time, clean thoroughly with water.

10 The best thing now is to paint the entire keel with a rust-converter and wash afterwards. Repeat as often as necessary.

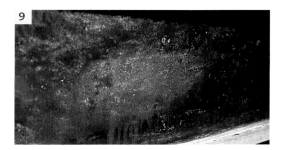

even be able to get at the underside of the keel. Having said that, the whole operation becomes considerably more difficult with centreboards or lifting keels which have to be dismantled and removed from the boat so you can reach and treat every single part. This means a lot of extra work, and perhaps the use of a crane or jack, but it's the only way to do it. While you're at it, you should also check the pulleys, bolts and lifting mechanisms as well. The other, more expensive but very sensible option is to have the centreboard serviced by a professional. Remove the centreboard completely and take it to a galvanising plant, where, after sandblasting, it can be immersed in a bath of zinc. This is by far the best form of protection and will help prevent iron centreboards rusting for many years; a galvanised coating is far tougher than any paint system.

Another method, assuming the keel has a fairly easy life, without too much chafe or friction from lifting mechanisms etc, is to cover it with fibreglass. Preparation is the same as before – which means removing all the rust and paint, and getting back to bare metal. This can be done manually or by sandblasting. You should then apply two layers of fibreglass mat with epoxy resin. Incidentally, it's absolutely vital that all the surfaces are completely encapsulated, otherwise water and

rust will start to creep in underneath. This is quite an intensive but also very thorough way of protecting keels which is why some of the more reputable builders now treat new boats using this particular method. After laminating two or three layers, the surface should be filled, faired and sanded. Take care not to damage the fibreglass by sanding into the mats. To be on the safe side, it's best to apply the filler fairly generously. The keel surface would then be painted four times with epoxy tar to complete the moisture barrier. After all that, assuming everything goes to plan, you can apply the antifouling in the certain knowledge that you won't have to worry about

11 Time to start building up a proper protective paint system. The first coat applied to the clean keel should be a two-pack base primer.

12 After the base primer has completely cured, you should apply a barrier coat. This establishes a chemical seal which will do much to help stop rust from forming again.

13 Here we see the sort of basic anti-rust coatings you might sensibly use: first, there's the rust-converter, then, next to it, the green barrier coating and finally, the two pots of paint that, when mixed together make up the first base primer.

14 After any necessary filling and fairing, you can now apply the antifouling. I would use a good, solvent-free, two-pot, water-based paint.

intended to keep the boat for a long time, the investment should eventually pay off because the boat would be worth a great deal more when you sold it.

A word about the joint between hull and keel. This is normally a problem-area because you're joining two different materials here, both with different thermal characteristics. Because of that, laminating would be entirely the wrong approach here. Between the keel and the wood or fibreglass hull it's vitally important to have a flexible layer of sealant at least three to five millimetres thick. When fitting the keel, liberally apply the silicone-free sealant and only lightly tighten the keel bolts. Only fully tighten them once the sealant has fully cured, then cut off any excess sealant that appears round the edge with a sharp knife.

your keel for many years to come.

You would, of course, have even less reason to worry if you decided to have your keel, centreboard, skeg or rudder made from less vulnerable materials – something which wouldn't rust or degrade in salt water. That would virtually eliminate all your corrosion problems once and for all. The real drawback, obviously, would be the cost. But if you

The silicone-free sealant can then be painted over along with the rest of the hull and keel. If the sealant contains silicone, however, painting is impossible.

In case you either can't or don't want to remove the keel, you should try and scrape the joint as best as you can. Clean it thoroughly, then fill the gap using a sealant gun.

Antifouling

The paint system on the bottom of your boat serves two main purposes: to protect the wood from water ingress and also to prevent marine organisms from attaching themselves to the hull.

To stop marine growth like algae and barnacles, it's essential to apply an effective form of antifouling, and renew it every year. For that reason, it's little wonder that the

1 After 20 years, the bottom of this boat looks like a moonscape. All the old layers must be stripped off before applying your new paint system.

accumulated layers of paint gets thicker and thicker over time. Even if you sand the bottom before painting it with a new coat of antifouling, you can never completely remove all the old layers underneath. On our Waarschip we found a veritable moonscape on the bottom of the boat; the whole area was

2 As long as the antifouling is still wet, you should clean the bottom with a high pressure hose immediately after the boat comes out of the water. It's probably easiest to remove the barnacles with a scraper.

3 Water dripping off the boat will have a high toxic content, and for that reason should be collected in a special container to stop it running back into the harbour. As a rule you should only use cranes that have adequate drains underneath, though that might not always be possible.

4 + 4a Small copper plates which are used as an alternative to antifouling paint. The entire bottom will be covered in panels like these, which can also be cut to fit round curved sections and tight radiuses. It's also a good osmosis prevention barrier.

4

4a

full of mountains and craters. To begin with, we removed as much as possible with a sharp scraper. A rough basic preparation like this is necessary before you start to remove the remaining paint with an orbital sander – and here, I would suggest you need a really powerful one with an efficient air suction attachment, otherwise the sandpaper really won't last very long at all. When all the paint has been removed, and you're back to the bare wood, you should inspect the timber itself in some detail to hunt out any signs of rot or mechanical damage. If you find any soft or moist spots, you should first dry them out thoroughly, if necessary using a hot air heater, then completely remove all the affected areas and fill with epoxy filler. When it's set, sand smooth and paint the underwater area of the hull with an epoxy sealer like Interprotect, which acts as a moisture barrier – applying two or three coats. You can use either a brush or roller, but for this job a brush may be preferable, because it means you can apply a slightly thicker film. After that, you should

5 Take a really good look in the bilge before starting work outside. Is it wet? If so, try to find where the water's coming from, and check for leaks, but examine the keel attachments as well.

6 If you find fine cracks in the paint or varnish, they will also be in the wood underneath. Each crack must be exposed and filled with epoxy to prevent further water ingress.

7 So many old layers of paint on top of each other don't provide a good basis for even more. That means removing them and getting back to bare wood, though it's an onerous job.

free. Whatever type you choose though, it's important to stay with one manufacturer's products, rather than mixing different systems.

Antifouling paint has changed over the years and will continue to evolve even though the problems remain much the same. As long as boats float in water, marine life will grow on them; barnacles and other organisms will also dramatically reduce the speed potential of any boat, so investing in an efficient form of antifouling makes a great deal of sense. And it's not just the hull we have to worry about. The efficiency of a propeller with growth on it can be reduced by up to 20 percent. Or to put it another way, it means the engine will have to consume one fifth more fuel – to reach the same speed as before –which makes a really big difference.

For all these reasons, we must make sure that the underwater area stays as clean as possible. In the past, this was achieved by using highly toxic paints with large quantities of poison or heavy metals. Not surprisingly, they were banned years ago for environmental reasons. Today, it's copper in various forms that stops marine growth. But this material too can be absorbed in the food chain, so scientists are continuing to look for

have a nice smooth surface on which to apply two coats of antifouling. The third and final coat can then be painted in the spring, shortly before launching the boat. There should be a time gap of at least 12 hours between painting and launching, but it can also be as long as three months. Some two-pot antifoulings can be mixed with water and are nearly solvent-

8 What do you do where the bottom and topside paint meet? If both areas are painted, you can sand them with a power tool, otherwise you must mask the topsides with tape and sand down by hand.

9 You should begin by removing all the loose layers mechanically, by hand – with a scraper. This is quite a lot easier and far less messy than using chemical strippers.

10 After removing all the loose paint you should then carry on with an orbital sander. But a word of warning: take special care not to sand too much into the wood itself.

alternative methods of preventing growth, which at the same time releases the smallest possible amounts of any harmful substance into the water.

In some sailing areas, especially on European inland lakes, all toxic antifoulings are banned completely. In such areas, extremely smooth surfaces – using Teflon for example – are sometimes used as alternatives, but the trouble is they don't work all the time. If all else fails, the only alternative is to clean the bottom at fairly short intervals, using either an underwater cleaning device or a good old high pressure cleaner while the boat is sitting in the hoist.

So do make sure you check out what kind of antifouling paint is allowed in your chosen area. If you're not sure, ask the local sailing club or try the coastguard.

One ancient and well tried and tested method designed to prevent fouling is to sheath the underwater sections with copper. Now, the idea has surfaced again in new forms. In fact, the marine industry has developed two ways of applying a protective coat of copper to your boat.

The first is a mixture of copper dust and epoxy resin which you put on, using several layers, over a clean primer on the underwater section of the hull. After the mixture has cured, the surface is lightly sanded immediately before launching to expose the copper particles. This surface will be effective for several years; all you have to do is lightly sand it from time to time.

The second method is to glue copper in tiny patches to the hull. This particular system was developed in the UK and has the

11 If you lose your concentration, you can quickly damage the paint on the topsides. So, for safety's sake it's probably better to sand this area by hand even if it takes a little longer.

12 Don't try to paint a straight line with a brush; it's not worth the risk. The best thing to do is to mask the area with tape first but then remove it immediately afterwards.

13 Two coats of primer should be followed by three layers of antifouling. If the surface is too rough, apply a couple of filler coats in between; we used something called Interfill – but always go for a reputable product.

14 The last lap. I recommend a good quality, two-pot system – which should help stave off any marine growth and keep the hull clean during the season.

advantage that the surface is about 80 percent metallic. The thin copper sheathing consists of tiny plates of copper mounted between two, self-adhesive foils. Rather like fitting a carpet at home, the pieces are cut to size with a knife and simply pressed on to the hull once the rear foil has been peeled off to expose the glue. And when the copper has been firmly stuck to the clean hull, the front foil can be removed to expose the metal plates beneath. The surface is then faired with a thin film of epoxy filler to close the tiny gaps between the copper plates themselves. Finally, the surface is lightly sanded or rinsed off with thinners.

The advantages of both methods are that each treatment should last for a number of years, making the annual antifouling paint job a thing of the past. Furthermore, the amount of copper released into the water is minimal. As an added bonus, these sheathings are nearly a hundred percent watertight and will therefore help prevent osmosis in fibreglass boats, or rot in boats built of timber. Of course, at the end of the day though, the final choice is up to you.

Shatterproof windows

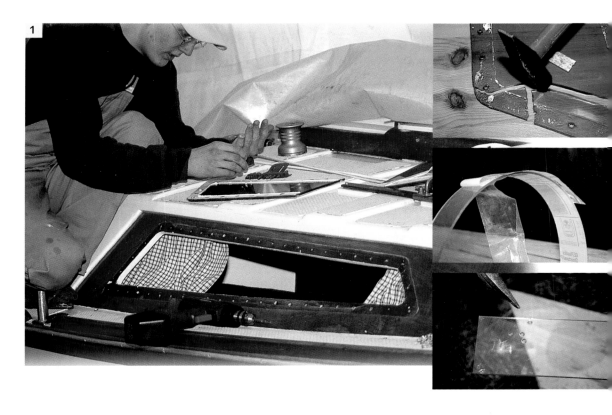

Perspex windows have one major drawback. Over time, they become brittle and crack. There's no such problem with Lexan, which makes it a better alternative.

1 Lexan is a very strong and flexible material and has performed well in tests, which makes it highly suitable for boat windows.

As with most things, the key to ultimate success often lies in choosing the right materials. This certainly applies to windows which, apart from anything else are extremely important components on any boat – not least from a safety point of view. A weakness here can cause all kinds of problems, particularly on passage in heavy weather. Boats have been lost because windows have either been smashed by big seas or damaged during knockdowns – so it's essential that you use the right material and, equally important,

make sure it's correctly fastened and secured. By the same token, scratched or faded windows can seriously degrade your boat's appearance, so, for all those reasons, in my judgement, the transparent plastic material known as Lexan, and marketed by General Electric Plastics, makes obvious sense. When struck with a hammer, in test conditions, for example, a standard Perspex window shatters into hundreds of splinters. Lexan, on the other hand, shows incredible resistance even when subjected to really heavy blows. Moreover, this transparent material is easy to bend and equally easy to saw and to drill. All of which makes it ideal for boats.

The first step is to remove the old, cracked windows. Don't forget to collect all the screws because you can use them again later. With a bit of luck, and assuming you're careful, you should be able to remove the old windows in one piece, in which case you can then use them as templates later on. On the other hand, if things don't go according to plan, you'll have to make new templates from strong cardboard.

Next, take a sharp knife, and clean all the sealant from the area around the window opening before sanding the sides of the timber coachroof. Unless you're using paint, coat with varnish and thinners, sand lightly again, and apply more varnish – up to eight coats is usually recommended. Put the varnish on with a roller, then lightly brush immediately afterwards. While the varnish eventually dries, you can cut out the new windows. You can even use the old windows as a template for drilling the holes. Use a 90-degree countersink for the screw-heads.

Now, with the window temporarily held in place with a few screws, you can cover the edges with masking tape. Then liberally coat the rim with sealant, which should preferably be silicone-free. Put the window in place and insert and tighten the screws, working your way outwards from the middle.

Sometimes old Perspex or Plexiglass windows can be saved. You can't do much about cracks, but dull or scratched windows can often be polished to make them clear once more. Use sanding paste and a very slow speed polishing head so you don't heat up the surface at all. That's really the only way to do it. If the surface begins to warm up, the whole job will be ruined. Use only light pressure and check the temperature of the surface by hand at frequent intervals. Finally, clean the surface with a good quality polishing paste and rub down to make it bright and clear.

2 A new window made from Lexan. This particular synthetic material is often also used to make protective shields on large industrial machines and is highly durable. As an added bonus, it's fitted with a scratchproof surface on the outside. The protective foil on the material shows you which side is which.

3 To save time, you can use an electric drill to screw in the cross-head screws. It's best to screw in simple screws by hand though. Otherwise, it's too easy to slip off the screw, which can result in damage that might be expensive to repair.

4 Remove the old window with as much care and patience as possible. Remember that you want to keep it in one piece, if that's at all practicable, so you can then use it as a template.

5 These dark stains and discolorations show where water has come in between the window and the cabin side. Leaks like this can cause problems later on, so this is an urgent matter.

6 Remove all the old sealant so you can sand the surfaces.

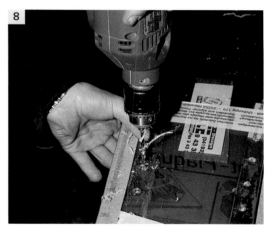

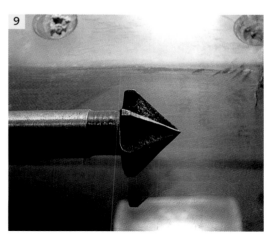

7 It's best to use an orbital sander when removing all the old varnish. You should then prime the surface with thinned varnish and later, when it's thoroughly dry, apply six to eight coats of varnish on top.

8 As you can see in this shot, the old and the new window have been securely taped together. This is a useful strategy and means it's possible to drill the screw holes with a normal drill.

9 Using a counter-sink. This will enlarge the holes so the screw heads will fit flush with the surface.

Using aerosol paint to give a fresh new look: plastic windows which are simply screwed to the outside of the cabin sides rarely look as elegant as windows held captive in an aluminium frame. On the other hand, they can be every bit as strong – and at least you can always improve their appearance. To make a start, sand the outer rim of the window, then mask the clear area, and spray the rim with an aerosol paint – a silver colour used for wheel-rims on cars usually works best, and really looks like an alloy frame. The spraying is best done with the window dismantled and taken home to the workshop, otherwise large areas of the cabin sides, deck and topsides will have to be masked off to protect against unwanted spray.

Next, an effective makeover with the help of anodising: old window frames often lose their original, attractive appearance and look dull and scratched. Mechanical damage by sheets or blocks may be the cause, but corrosion between the stainless steel screws and alloy frame can also cause problems. Either way, new anodising techniques can help to restore the frame to its former glory. However, it can only be done by a specialist company. Refurbishing the frame, once it's been taken off the boat, means removing the old layer of anodising, cleaning the frame

10 At this stage, you should fix the window in place temporarily with just a few screws so the edges can be covered with masking tape.

11 Now you can start applying the sealant and fitting the window in place. Press and insert the screws, beginning in the middle and working your way outwards. All the air bubbles should be completely removed.

12 After a day's curing time, you can simply pull off the excess sealant together with the masking tape. If, by chance, anything should be left on the window, carefully scrape it off with a plastic spatula.

itself, then anodising again. You can even choose the colour, or decide whether you want the frame to be glossy or matt.

A new look with new frames: sometimes, when corrosion between screws and frames have significantly weakened the whole assembly, it's simply impossible to remove the old frames at all – the screws often simply shear off when you try to unscrew them. In that case the only thing you can do is replace the whole window.

If the manufacturer of the original window is still in business, you might be able to find a new one that fits exactly. If not, it's a question of opting for a marginally larger one. After all, in most cases, it's not too difficult to slightly enlarge the opening in the cabin sides. It's also theoretically possible to reduce the size of the opening but this is a complex and difficult operation. The last and most expensive but also the easiest option is of course to have the entire window refurbished by a professional. With every job, it's a question of priorities. Sometimes it's best to do everything yourself; sometimes you can save time, if not actual money, by calling in an expert. It all depends which areas of the boat you feel most comfortable working with. What might be easy for one person can be a real challenge for another.

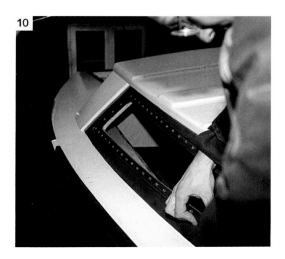

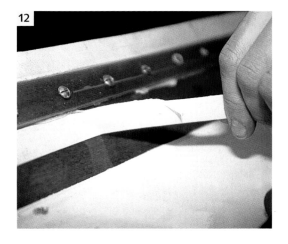

Fitting hatches

If you want to fit a new hatch because the old one is defective, you'll also need to make a new base frame, which sits between the curved deck and the hatch itself.

1 Structural integrity is all important, so the wooden frame needs to be sufficiently strong. Otherwise, the surrounding deck will flex.

Hatches should be both watertight and strong enough to be walked and stood on. They should also have a mechanism which allows you to close them securely. It's hardly worth making your own hatch these days, because you can buy quite good ones for as little as about £130 ($230) – and they come in a wide range of sizes. It goes without saying that you should try and find a new hatch that has more or less the same dimensions as the one you're replacing.

I decided on a Vetus hatch made from alloy that nearly but not quite fitted the opening in the deck. To make the final adjustment, I built a massive mahogany frame which made up the difference. The height of the frame depends on the curvature of the deck. In practice, therefore, you have to shape the underside of the frame to fit, using either a hacksaw or a file. You don't have to work with absolute precision here because the frame will simply be bonded to the deck with thickened epoxy resin. This is good not only

2 Epoxy is a wonderful material for the amateur renovator. It bonds extremely well, can be thickened with various additives to suit different purposes, is easy to work with, and highly resistant and durable. It's available in various quantities – and for that reason alone, you should always keep a small repair pack on board.

3 A wide timber frame like this one not only sits comfortably on the curved fibreglass deck but also strengthens it to prevent any flexing. All hatches must be both strong and secure.

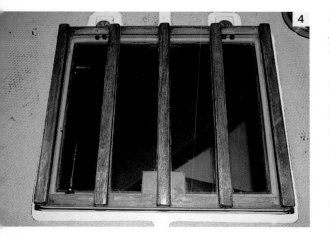

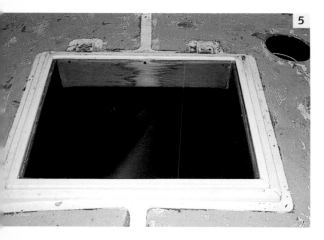

for bonding but also for filling any of the tiny gaps that might remain between deck and hatch frame.

When the first application of epoxy has cured, apply another fillet around the base of the frame. Leave to cure, then sand down. Finally, the wooden frame should be primed and varnished three or four times. Only then should you fit the hatch – after coating the underside of its frame with silicone sealant then screwing in place. Don't tighten the screws too much, otherwise too much sealant will be forced out from between the hatch frame and the wooden surround. Too little sealant left between the alloy hatch and the timber frame could cause problems. Because the two materials have different thermo-dynamic characteristics, when they start to expand or contract, the hatch will inevitably start to leak along the frame.

Should the hatch be fitted so it opens forward, over the bows, or faces backwards, towards the stern? It's a common question but, I'm afraid, there's no simple answer. A hatch that opens at the front (facing the bows) will provide much better ventilation when the boat is lying at anchor. On the other hand, you couldn't leave it open, even slightly, as soon as it started to rain. In wet weather a hatch that opened towards the stern would be more practical, because you could open it a touch and still remain dry.

How you decide for yourself in the end is probably very much a matter of personal taste – though many production yachts seem to fit forward-opening hatches these days. The most important priority, in my view, concerns safety. You should only fit one which can be opened wide enough to let you enter and leave the forepeak – particularly in an emergency.

Either way, when you go shopping for a new hatch, try and find a good quality product and examine it carefully. Can you remove the rubber seal? If it's worn, damaged or brittle, is it easy to buy a spare? The mechanism which keeps the hatch open should also be well designed. It seems a really good idea to have a hatch which is held in position by friction, because it can be opened and held at any angle. The design of the securing levers is also vitally important; above all, they should be quick and easy to use. Similarly, there's a real practical advantage in having a hatch which can be closed and secured when you're on deck.

In general, the same rule we applied to fitting the windows holds good here as well. If you want to fit a new hatch, try to get one that's slightly larger than the old one. It may also be possible to fit a smaller one but that can be quite tricky because, of course, you'll have to reduce the size of the opening in the deck.

The next important consideration is how to make sure that the wooden frame on which the hatch is screwed is absolutely even. It's crucial, because otherwise, when its positioned in place, the alloy frame will end up slightly twisted and the hatch will almost certainly leak from day one. And another thing: don't make the wooden frame too thin. A hatch should be extremely strong – but so should the timber structure that holds it in place.

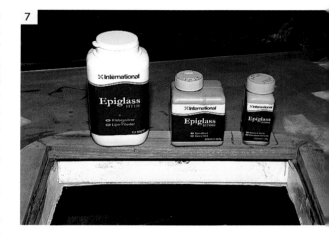

4 This old hatch is no longer watertight and doesn't look too strong either. To make matters worse, the wooden frame is also too thin and too flexible to really cope with the forces at work here.

5 As you can see only too clearly here, this inadequate and flimsy form of construction has already let in a great deal of water. The frame is also damaged in the corners.

6 This hatch was chosen with reference to the size of the deck opening. In fact, it's a bit bigger, so the chunky new frame will form a large base.

7 The new frame with the underside roughly shaped to fit the curvature of the deck. It should be bonded with a good quality epoxy resin, hardener and additive.

8 Mix resin and hardener to a ratio of 4:1. Stick an old tape measure into a glass, pour in resin to a depth of four centimetres, then add hardener until the level reaches five centimetres.

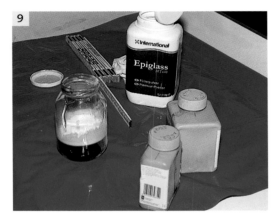

10 To find the right consistency it's largely a matter of trial and error. Simply keep on adding the powder carefully, in small doses, until the thickness seems right.

11 Liberally apply the mixture to the frame and deck with a brush, and press the frame in place. When the epoxy starts to go off, remove any of the excess which will have been squeezed out from between the frame and the deck.

12 Now's the time to check that everything fits properly. Make sure the hatch frame sits evenly and snugly on the wooden frame without any gaps.

13 Once the wooden frame has been varnished or painted, apply silicone sealant to the hatch frame, and screw in place, taking care not to squeeze too much from between the hatch and the deck frame.

9 Stir well, and add small amounts of the white thickening powder to end up with a thick mixture that can still be applied with a brush.

Painting the hull

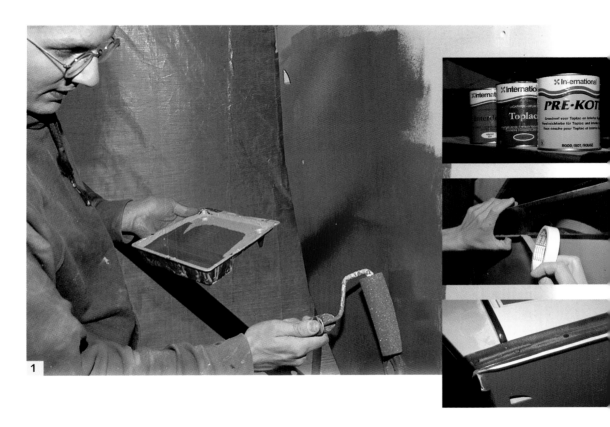

1

After all the hard work and preparation, we're ready at last to apply the final gloss. The paint you use is best applied with a foam roller and a brush.

1 There are numerous brands to choose from. This is a typical one-pot system: grey primer, light red undercoat and bright red topcoat.

This is the moment you've been waiting for. After all the many hours of preparation, it's time to apply that shiny new coat of gloss paint. It's an exciting time but you should avoid the obvious temptation to rush in because it's critical at this stage that the working environment is absolutely right. Wherever you choose to carry out the refit, when it comes to painting, the conditions must be completely dust-free. Adequate

2 One-pot paint may not be as sophisticated as two-pot but can give you a really good finish. In fact, if the job has been done well, the boat should look as if it's been sprayed.

3 Sanding, sanding, sanding. After each coat, lightly sand down with 400 Grade 'Wet or Dry' which should be used wet. But remember, you should always clean the paper thoroughly in between. After sanding, wipe the surface down and make sure it's dry. After that you should remove any dust with a tack-cloth or dust tissue.

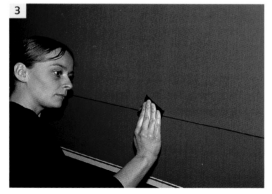

lighting is also important; daylight is best. The temperature should be between 15 and 20 degrees Celsius and you should have enough room to move easily round the boat. Only in these sort of conditions, can you expect to do a really good job. Having said that, it's good to know that today's products not only give good results but can be applied by amateurs like us – as long as we've prepared everything properly and follow a few simple guidelines.

The final coat should be applied once the hull has been filled, faired, sanded and primed twice (one coat of grey primer and one coat of red undercoat) – and once you've made sure that the hull is free of scratches and dust.

You can't use the paint straight from the tin; it should be poured into a tray, because you'll now be working with both a foam roller and a flat brush. For the best result it's good to have two people; one applying a generous coat of paint with the foam roller, the second then following up afterwards smoothing the wet paint over with the brush to give a nice, even finish.

It's quite a delicate job, because the consistency of the paint is all important and you need to get it right. In other words, you shouldn't apply the paint too thinly (it won't flow properly otherwise), but not too thickly either (in which case it will run too much).

If you're still experimenting, don't be in too much of a hurry to start on the hull. It might be a much better idea to start with the transom instead. Then, if, for any reason, you don't get a good result, you can always sand it down and start again. And a word of warning: don't ever be tempted to try and apply more

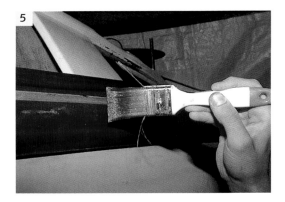

4 Here we have an extremely well sanded surface. As we've said before, this is the best basis for a decent paint job. The first coat of varnish should be applied with 30 percent thinners. After that, you should sand down again.

5 It's a good idea to apply at least three, but not more than eight coats of varnish to get the right kind of build-up. Always treat the rubbing strake with extra care.

6 When all the varnishing has been completed, you can finally begin on the hull. That means filling, priming and undercoating before finally applying two layers of topcoat.

7 Once the varnish has cured completely, you should cover it thoroughly with masking tape. Use a smooth tape so the paint won't run underneath it and spoil the edge.

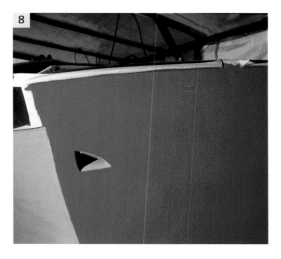

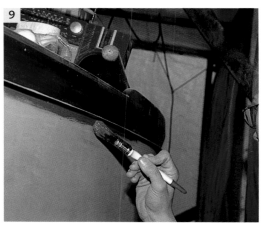

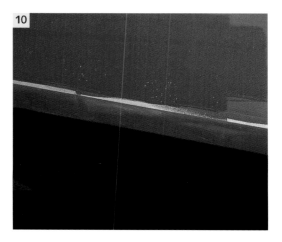

8 Don't rush in too quickly, but take your time and begin with the transom, particularly if you're still experimenting. This is a small area that can fairly easily be re-done should anything go wrong.

9 It's always best to begin in the corners and then paint over the varnish. Corners should be treated with particular care to prevent any water getting in later on.

10 It's virtually impossible to achieve a straight line without masking tape. Remove the tape as soon as the paint begins to dry. If you leave it too long, you'll find it hard to remove.

paint on a coat that's been applied too thinly and is still wet; it's almost bound to go wrong. If you want absolute perfection, or at least as close as you can get to it, you should think about applying two final coats anyway, but not unless you sand down lightly in between.

Another critical decision you'll have to make is whether to use one-pot or two-pot paint. It's not really the case that one is 'better' than the other; the systems have different characteristics – so, in the end, it all depends what you want.

A one-pot paint is particularly convenient because, as the name implies, it comes ready to use in the tin. You can add up to ten per cent thinners if necessary, stir well, and begin to paint straight away. This paint will start to go off after a few hours; it will also be dust-dry and cure overnight. The warmer the environment, the quicker this kind of paint will dry.

The two-pot system, on the other hand, needs to be prepared first, by mixing the contents of the two pots, the paint and the hardener. Like polyester or epoxy resin, it won't react or cure without the hardener which, in fact is a good description of it because the paint itself doesn't so much dry, as harden. Again, the warmer the environment, the quicker the reaction time.

11 The all-important final coat. We decided to use a high gloss topcoat on our boat. Again, as already indicated, it's best to begin in the corners using a brush.

12 The paint should then be applied with a foam roller. Always try to spread the paint as slowly and evenly as possible to avoid trapping too many air bubbles.

13 Smoothing the paint. Immediately after the paint has been applied with the roller, smooth over with a perfectly clean, flat brush to remove bubbles. Only apply very light pressure and always smooth out horizontally.

The main difference between the two is that one-pot paint will dry, but always stay slightly flexible. That makes it more suitable for traditional, wooden boats whose planks are always on the move. Also, the paint is more resistant to small bumps and knocks. Finally, it's considerably simpler to apply because it flows more easily. On the other hand, it's not quite as durable as two-pot paint.

Two-pot is also much more difficult to apply, so it takes more practice to do a decent job. But once it's actually on, it provides a very hard and long lasting surface. It's not quite as hard as the gelcoat but can last nearly as long. It's only suitable for plywood, fibreglass or steel; not for traditional planked timber because, as already intimated, it's not sufficiently elastic. The pot life of two-pot paint depends on the temperature of your surroundings, and it's important to only mix enough paint to use in one go, before it starts to go off. And always complete one part of the hull after the other; apply the paint with a roller and immediately smooth with a brush or a foam pad. Don't hang around too long because the paint will quickly begin to go off. Should the paint have been applied too thickly so it's started to run, sand with 1000 Grade paper once it's properly cured, then polish.

Protecting the deck

A timber deck needs plenty of protection – from sunlight, salt water and general wear and tear. That's why it's so important to choose a tough and durable finish – and to make sure you apply it with care.

This plywood deck was coated with a layer of cork and rubber. It has fairly good anti-slip properties but over the years, the sheathing has faded and the edges de-laminated from the deck. For that reason, we wanted to remove it and use a special anti-slip deck paint instead.

But first, we had to tackle the varnish or

1 However tempted you may be, don't rip the old deck sheathing off with brute force, otherwise you may damage the deck underneath.

brightwork which was taken right back to bare wood, then sanded smooth and treated to between six and eight coats of varnish. It always makes sense to begin with the varnished timber like this, because it can be masked off with tape to make sure you end up with very clearly defined edges to the paint.

This is how we tackled the various stages of the operation. First we removed all the deck fittings, then we took off the old

2

3

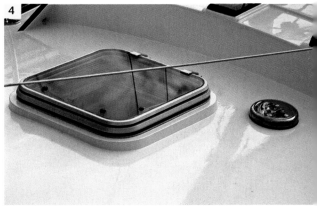

4

2 If you want to lead the halyards and other lines aft to make them easier to reach, you must first make wooden blocks for all the necessary fittings. This is the kind of improvement that can make your boat less stressful to handle and is ideally done while you're carrying out a major refit like this.

3 Clean edges. Always finish off the varnished areas first, then do the painting. Varnish should overlap the areas you want to paint by a few millimetres. The varnish will later be over-painted but in the process, you should establish a good seal and avoid getting cracks in the paint.

4 New hatch, new ventilators. New fittings like this look good on deck and will really enhance your boat's appearance. But don't place them too close to each other – it gives a rather amateurish appearance and can ruin the overall effect.

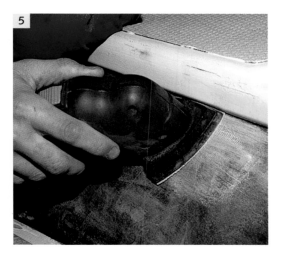

sheathing with a chisel and scraper. Be extremely careful when you're doing this, because, if the bonding is still good in places, it's incredibly easy to damage the plywood underneath. Similarly, you might end up with odd spots of old glue on deck, but all that can later be sanded off with an orbital sander. If there's any damage to the outer layer of the plywood, you can easily repair it with epoxy resin. Fill the damaged area with epoxy, cover with a plastic foil kept in place with something suitably heavy and wide. After it's cured, fill the deck with epoxy filler, leave to cure and sand down with 180-Grade paper.

5 Once the fittings have been removed (carefully label them all) start sanding the wood. For a thorough job, and to avoid damage, use a small sander for the corners.

6 Large areas can be sanded with an orbital disc sander until the wood is bare. Old varnish stands out against new varnish, so remove every trace of it before you apply the first coat.

7 Be careful when removing the sheathing. If the adhesive is still hanging on in places, it can tear off the top layer of plywood. Damaged areas like these should be sealed and faired with epoxy resin.

8 After filling, it's time to sand it all down again. Where necessary, you should then fill again, in case the material has shrunk during the curing process leaving dips and dents in the surface.

9 These are the most difficult areas. Small corners like this can only be sanded by hand. It's a good idea to wrap the sanding paper around a small batten to reach into the corners.

After sanding, you should cover the deck with two coats of primer and three coats of deck paint.

For a better appearance, you can always coat the cabin sides and coachroof with something bright and glossy, and only paint anti-slip areas where you actually need them.

When conducting a thorough refit, you should take the opportunity to reorganise the deck layout more efficiently. After all, one of the big developments in recent years has been the use of specialised gear and equipment to make sail handling easier. For example, you could lead the halyards back to the cockpit, install new ventilators or exchange the hatch for a bigger or better one. You can easily draw up a plan by photocopying and enlarging the deck drawing from the original brochure. That way, you can work out where everything goes before you actually start.

However, remember that whatever arrangements you may be planning on deck, it's important to think about what's happening to the same area below. At the very least, you should be able to reach the components you've just fitted. For example, if you plan to mount a new ventilator, make sure it doesn't sit on top of a bulkhead! And if you're adding new deck fittings, the deck itself might have to be strengthened in the relevant area by inserting a plywood backing pad underneath the fitting. That's particularly important if you're leading the halyards back to the cockpit, which also entails fitting new winches, jammers and the like. They should be supported by an additional 14 millimetre pad of marine plywood and be bonded beneath the deck with thickened epoxy resin, making sure it sits snugly beneath the deck, without any gaps between the wood and the deck itself.

Perhaps you also want to replace the genoa tracks; if so, this is the ideal time to do it. First, make sure you can reach all the bolts from below. Some yards fit a complete deck to the hull without thinking about how you might carry out repairs or refits later on. In some cases, parts of the interior will have to be cut away in order to get at the bolts. If so, you also have to repair it afterwards.

If you find small areas of rot in a wooden deck, remove all the soft spots and let the wood dry out completely. You can then fill the gap with thickened epoxy resin, before sanding and painting.

The same problem is less easy to deal with if the area is varnished rather than painted because varnish shows every mark underneath. However, small spots can always be filled with epoxy resin mixed with tiny wood shavings from the same type of wood. If the area is bigger, it's best to insert a new piece of wood, but check carefully (by wetting the bare timber) that the colour will match the surrounding wood when you varnish it.

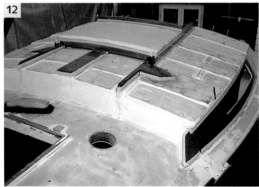

10 All the wooden parts will have to be thoroughly sanded. If you want to do a proper job, those bits you want to varnish should be taken right back to the bare wood.

11 This wood is bare and clean and ready for the first coat. Apply the initial layer of varnish mixed with about 50 percent thinners to help it penetrate deep into the fibres of the timber.

12 When all the wooden parts have been varnished, mask and protect them with tape; you should then clean the deck with a brush and a vacuum cleaner to remove any traces of dirt or dust.

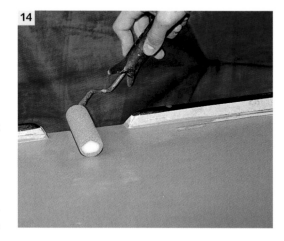

13 Use a flat brush for the corners and a foam roller for the bigger, open areas. Grey primer provides a base for the first coat of paint. You should apply either two or three layers.

14 It's important to make sure that the paint reaches right into the corners, otherwise they can end up as problem areas and allow moisture in which can cause problems later.

16 The cockpit after its first layer of paint. Always paint the inner surfaces too, as well as the various nooks and crannies you'll find in every cockpit.

17 Depending on the type of boat, it might be necessary to dismantle certain parts in order to reach into awkward corners. If you don't paint or varnish them, it can ruin the whole paint job.

18 As soon as the paint begins to go off, remove the masking tape. If you leave it too long, it will be difficult to remove and some of it will remain on the varnish.

19 Here it is! The old deck looking all bright and shiny. It now has several layers of paint which need time to cure completely, even if the surface is already dry. Wait for a few days before putting the fittings back on.

15 Not a popular job, but a necessary one. Sanding between layers of paint. After the first coat you can clearly see where the surface is still rough and where it needs to be sanded.

Fitting lockers and frames

Open storage spaces don't just look out of place on a yacht; if things fall out as soon as the boat starts to heel, they can actually be dangerous too. This is how you can quickly convert an open shelf into a proper seagoing storage space.

1 This is the conservative or classic look: white doors, with dark mahogany frames. It's a traditional and extremely practical way to decorate a boat's interior and to make old and scruffy surfaces look good again.

2 Stowage in the quarter-berth. Again, white is the best colour in a confined area like this, because it lights up dark corners and creates a feeling of space.

3 Every available nook and cranny should be used for storage especially on smaller yachts. These particular lockers above the berth were fitted later; they don't steal any room from the berth but provide additional space.

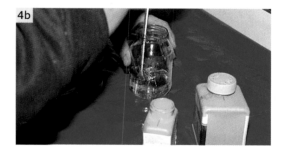

4 Fitting new wooden fronts to improve the look of old lockers. You can use the old door as a base.

4a + 4b Cramps and epoxy.

Stowage space is always at a premium, especially on smaller boats. It's a good idea, therefore, to make the best possible use of all the available space. For instance, lockers in the saloon, which will probably be in constant use, should fulfil the following criteria: they should be sensibly designed – which, above all, means not too big. If your lockers are too deep, for example, it's all too easy to lose things in the bottom. They should also have a secure hatch that can be opened and closed with one hand and which stays shut even in the roughest weather. And, last but not least,

5

the fronts should look smart and attractive, as well. It sounds a tall order but in many cases, it's not that difficult to achieve.

I've chosen somewhat traditional hatch openings for the lockers in the saloon. The frontal areas and doors are made of plywood, painted white, and are surrounded by glossy, richly varnished mahogany frames. Even the ring around the finger hole for the catch makes use of contrasting dark wood.

If, as was the case here, you already have adequate and secure lockers in the saloon – which don't need replacing, all you need to do is renew the front locker doors. You can do that easily by simply bonding on new fronts. The first step would be to make templates from cardboard, then cut out the new wooden fronts and stick them to the old locker doors with epoxy resin. Then, of course, you have to

5 Stowage in the saloon. Lockers with doors can be closed for security even in heavy weather. Open storage, though, must be deep and fitted with a high fiddle so that nothing can fall out even if the boat is heeled. Shallow boards with small fiddles are only useful for books.

re-cut the old openings with a hacksaw to make sure they fit the new doors. You then cut the mahogany frame and bond it to the door with epoxy. The next stage is to mount the hinges and see how everything fits together. Only when the doors are precisely right, and open and close without effort, should you begin varnishing and painting. The very last step is to cut the holes for the securing mechanisms and to mount them as well.

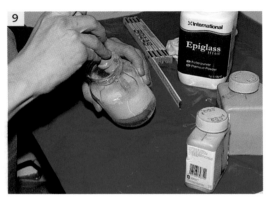

6 Before we got to work. It's not particularly attractive and hardly practical. The loose doors have no hinges but have to be removed completely when you open them.

7 If you can still use the locker, you don't have to remove it; instead, you can simply fit a new front on top. Make a cardboard template to help you cut the wood to the right shape.

8 Once you're sure that the template is OK, you can use it to cut out the new locker doors. We used good quality 10 millimetre marine ply for strength and durability.

9 To bond the new fronts, we used four parts of a good quality epoxy resin to one part hardener adding thickening additive a little at a time. We wanted an epoxy paste that could still just about be applied with a brush.

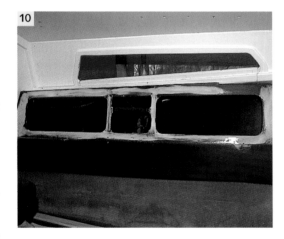

10 As always, preparation is vitally important. Once the surface has been thoroughly sanded and cleaned, the epoxy can be applied. Make sure you spread it nice and evenly with the brush.

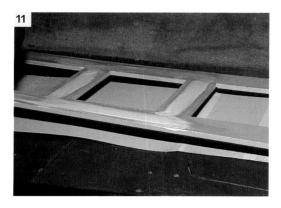

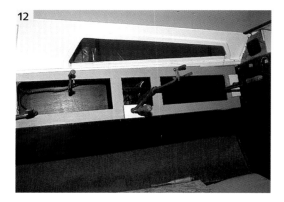

12 To achieve the firm and even pressure you need to make a decent bond, it's a good idea to place small pieces of wood between the fixing cramps and the locker front, like this.

13 After a while, you should tighten the fixing cramps and, assuming it's still wet and uncured, immediately remove any excess epoxy with a cloth. If it dries, it's extremely difficult to remove.

14 Once the epoxy has cured completely, you need to trim the old openings to size. To do that, you could use a hacksaw. The next step is to sand the edges until smooth.

15 The first dummy run. The frame should fit into the opening snugly and without the need for too much force. Having got this far, it makes sense to number both frames and openings.

11 The new locker fronts. At this stage of the operation they've already been carefully painted with primer, having been evenly coated with epoxy on the back and then glued into position.

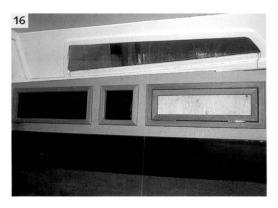

16 The new locker doors before the final touches. Every part will be painted with white gloss, apart from the frames which will be picked out in varnish to provide an attractive contrast.

17 Cutting the angles with the mitre-jig. The better the tools, the better the result. If you plan to make a lot of locker fronts, it might be useful to have an electric saw with a proper jig.

18 Having checked the fit to make sure you've got everything right, you should coat the corners with epoxy. Once again, cramps have been used to hold the bonding in place.

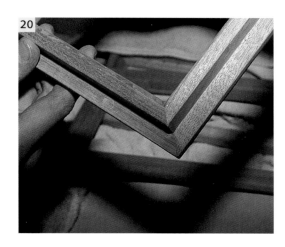

19 If you don't have suitable cramps, you can always improvise, and hold the bonding in place with several layers of tape. Epoxy resin doesn't need that much pressure to bond well.

20 Here we have a precise 90-degree corner. To save any unnecessary mistakes, it's a good idea to make a few test cuts with your mitre jig to ensure the kind of accuracy that's needed here.

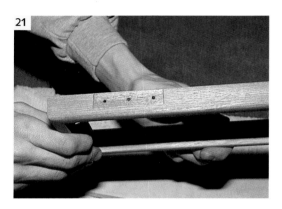

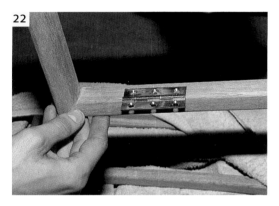

22 If you want the door to fold down to 180 degrees, the hinges must be fastened accordingly, otherwise the door won't fold down far enough. The axis of the hinge must be just outside the front face.

23 Check the final fit of all the doors before varnishing (or painting). If you want to make it easier, use strap hinges which are easier to fit than individual hinges.

24 Cover and protect. Apply the first coat of varnish which should be mixed with 40 to 50 percent thinners, then sand again, remove the dust, and add three to four coats of varnish using a flat brush.

21 Fitting the hinges is somewhat less easy because you have to carefully cut out the indent with a chisel. You don't want to make a mistake here, so practice first, and take your time.

25 Here's a useful tip if you want to varnish both sides of the doors in one go. Screw some small wooden screws into the back; the wet door can rest on them while they dry.

Repairing damaged timber

Wood that dries out too much will sometimes split and crack. However, it's not really such a big problem; small cracks can easily be repaired with epoxy, filler and fibreglass.

Sometimes cracks will show up even in new timber. It's fairly common during a hot, dry summer, or after the first winter lay-up ashore. The reason is usually straightforward: it means the builders failed to make sure the

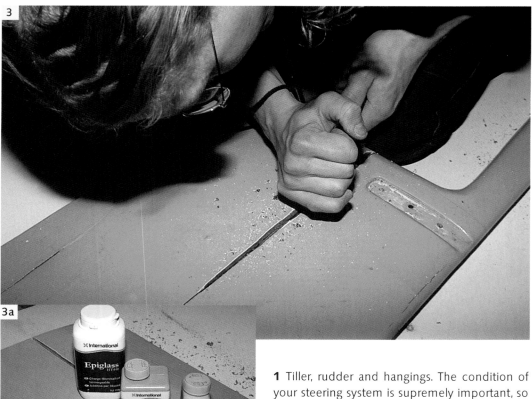

1 Tiller, rudder and hangings. The condition of your steering system is supremely important, so if you make any changes, make sure you don't compromise on safety or strength.

2 Yachts of every size and type are subjected to severe forces at sea. A refit should actually make the boat stronger and more seaworthy. If you're in doubt about anything, seek the professional advice of a surveyor.

3 + 3a + 3b You don't have to be a skilled craftsman. Thanks to modern materials, it's easy, even for an amateur, to repair cracked and split timber.

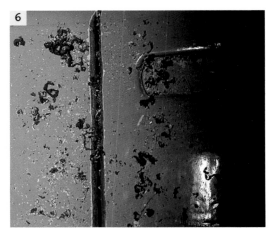

wood was completely dry before they used it. What happens then, as soon as it begins to dry and lose moisture, is that it shrinks, which can also cause it to split. On our boat, the side supports of the rudder were cracked. But happily, the repair was simple and quick.

We began by opening up the crack with a scraper, to make it even bigger, so we could reach the core of the wood. This also meant that, at a later stage we could eliminate any air bubbles from underneath the epoxy. Then we sanded the adjacent areas (about 15 centimetres on either side of the crack) with 150-Grade paper.

After the preparation we could start making a proper repair. We cut two strips of fibreglass mat, each about 20 centimetres wide. Then we mixed up some epoxy resin with hardener and covered the entire crack inside with it. The next step was to fill the gap with even more epoxy, but this time, we thickened it up with additive to make a more substantial paste. Once this was properly cured, we mixed up yet more epoxy resin with hardener and applied it to the repair. The next stage was to apply the fibreglass strip to the repair and carefully paint on more resin with the brush until the strip was thoroughly saturated. After putting on the second strip, we applied more resin.

4 The builders used marine plywood for the core of this rudder blade but the supports were made of solid mahogany which, at the time, was probably too wet, and has now shrunk and split. Luckily it's fairly easy to repair.

5 After removing the fittings we opened up and slightly enlarged the crack with a V-shaped scraper. This is essential if you want the epoxy resin to penetrate right into the bottom of the crack.

6 The crack shown here was then cleaned with a hard brush so the epoxy could penetrate easily and find its way into every nook and cranny.

The following day, when the entire repair was well cured, the whole area was faired with filler until the structure of the fibreglass mat was completely hidden from view. It was then sanded and primed. Finally we added three coats of topcoat paint. This also acts as an all-important moisture barrier.

When repairing or refitting any component on a boat, try to think about the practical aspects. Ideally, the refurbished part should work better and have a greater margin of safety than it did before. Track down any weak spots and repair them. With regards to rigging and rudders, remember, these are highly critical areas. The same applies to the keel bolts, the rudder and its hangings, the tiller, the mast step and its support, and, of course, the mast itself. Plywood can quite easily rot so, if you find any on your boat, you should make a point of examining it closely to check out any soft or weak spots that might cause problems later on. If you do find any, you must remove them and make a repair with epoxy and fibreglass as already described.

Check the rigging with tremendous care; the safety of your boat and your crew can depend on it. Rigging screws may be corroded or bent, while rolled steel terminals can often get damaged. Wire rigging will be weakened

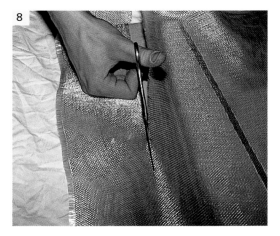

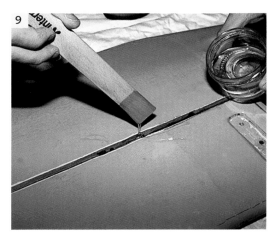

7 The adjoining areas (about 15 centimetres either side) were sanded down to provide a better surface for the epoxy laminate to adhere to. It's always important to make sure you get a decent bond.

8 The fibreglass mat was cut into strips with sharp scissors. We prepared two strips for each side of the rudder. When laying them in position, make sure that they overlap each other on both sides, as well as on the top and bottom.

9 The epoxy resin was then prepared (4 parts resin, one part hardener) and poured into the crack until it ran out of the ends.

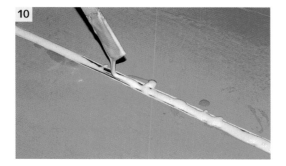

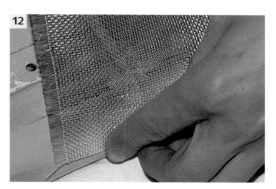

if damaged. Watch out for any broken strands sticking out like hooks from the wire itself. And where stainless steel and aluminium come into direct contact, you may find that corrosion has set in weakening the integrity of the metal – entire winches have been known to break free from the mast taking their steel mountings with them – all because of corrosion. As we've pointed out in other chapters, the use of dissimilar metals is often a cause for concern. If you're in any doubt, consult a professional and have the rigging checked by a qualified surveyor.

10 Putty was mixed with resin hardener and thickening additive, then inserted into the crack, taking care not to create too many air bubbles. The ends of the crack could be sealed off with tape.

11 The mixture began to go off shortly after the end of the pot life. This is the time to remove any excess epoxy with a wooden spatula, because it helps reduce sanding and fairing afterwards.

12 After the filling inside the crack had cured, we covered the strips along both sides with epoxy resin mixed with hardener. We then placed the fibreglass strip on top, taking care that it lay flat without any creases.

13 We applied more resin with a brush until the mat was completely transparent and saturated. Air bubbles were removed by dabbing them with a brush.

The perfect colour scheme

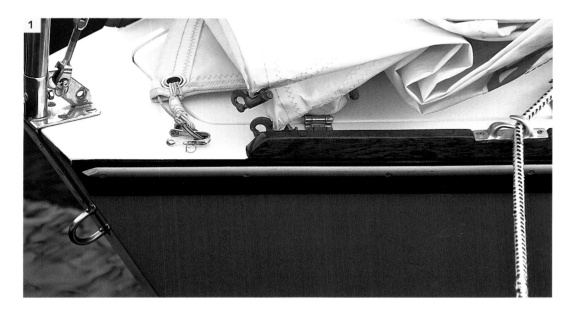

Firstly, paint should provide good protection for the hull and deck. But there's more to it than that. The visual impact of a new colour scheme can make a huge difference to the boat's appearance.

1 Red, white, mahogany and brass always go extremely well together. In practice, working out the most appropriate combinations of colours and materials is vital if you want the refit to be a success. Indeed, it's so important that it might even be a good idea to seek professional advice about different colour schemes.

The right choice of colours can change the appearance of a boat dramatically and turn it into a proper little yacht. With ours, we wanted to change two things. The area below decks was far too dark, while the deck itself, which was covered with panels of Polygrip, looked a bit like a patchwork quilt. Both made our small boat look even smaller. It's a common problem with older boats but there's a lot you can do to make things better.

To start with, below decks we painted many of the surfaces white, which lightened up the modest saloon and generally made everything look brighter and roomier. At the same time though, we retained a traditional nautical theme with hefty, varnished mahogany frames. On deck, large areas of white again made the boat look longer and cleaner. When it comes to choosing the colours, you must also decide whether you

want to use conventional one-pot paints or the more modern two-pot systems. One pot paints are unquestionably easy to use; they also have a softer surface and are suitable for solid timber. If the paint needs to be especially hard and durable, on plywood or fibreglass surfaces for example, then two-pot paint with hardener might be better, although admittedly, it's a bit more complicated to use. To start with, therefore, just paint a few tiny test areas to see how it goes.

Either way, you should only paint when the temperature is just right (not below ten degrees Celsius) and prepare the surface thoroughly (filling, fairing and sanding). Then apply the paint with a roller and smooth over with the brush immediately afterwards. Read the manufacturer's instructions – and any relevant literature that's available – and stick religiously to the recommended intervals between coats.

The picture sequence that follows shows how one-pot paint should be applied.

2a + 2b Using one-pot systems which are easier to apply and somewhat more flexible. The brands you opt for are a matter of personal choice.

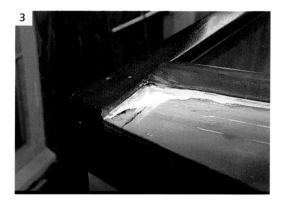

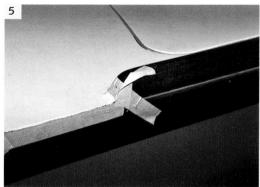

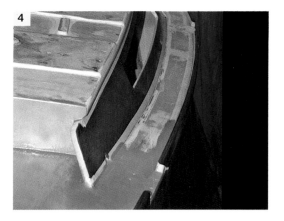

3 The right sequence is important. After sanding and cleaning, first varnish all the wooden parts with between five and eight coats, adding 50 percent thinners for the first coat.

4 Next, fill and fair all the deck areas; sand and mask the varnished parts and paint twice with primer. If necessary, fill again after the first coat of primer and sand once more. After the primer, apply three coats of paint.

5 Overlapping the varnish and paint. Spread a little varnish on the deck as well. Then mask the varnish when it's fully cured, leaving a 5-millimetre strip at the bottom.

6 Take care when varnishing or painting especially in sharp corners like these. Coatings can easily crack here, ruining an otherwise perfect job.

7 A perfect combination? The white deck and red hull provide a really nice and attractive contrast, while the varnished parts enhance the traditional boaty feel. The best of both worlds.

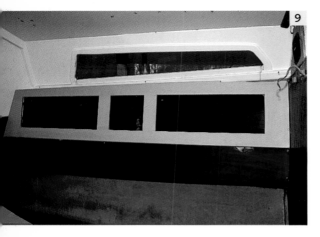

8 Dark interior surfaces, shown here before the refit, tend to make small cabins look even smaller. Using a lighter colour scheme can make a huge difference and create a feeling of space.

9 No one enjoys it, but proper preparation is vitally important. We sanded and primed our newly built locker fronts. To make a really neat job, the screws were countersunk and then finally filled.

10 The frames and locker fronts were varnished and painted separately. They were then re-fitted which meant adjusting the size of the opening.

As you probably realise, there are certain, well established colour combinations for boats, and there's no harm in following the norm. After all, they've stood the test of time. For example, brightly varnished mahogany always goes well with glossy white surfaces and bronze or brass fittings. Such elements also provide attractive contrasts. Deep red, blue or green will also blend in well with these sort of combinations, while, for some reason, yellow, brown, beige or grey somehow never seem to work, at least, not on boats, anyway.

Anyhow, before you finally make your mind up, if you're still planning your refit, why not copy the drawing from the boat's brochure a few times and try some alternative colour schemes? Professionals also use their computers to experiment with different colours, and you could always do the same. After all, repainting your boat will take a great amount of time and effort and you want to get it right. It would be a shame if the refit were ruined simply because you chose the wrong colours. Vertical stripes on a high freeboard hull, for example, will make the boat seem even tubbier, while horizontal stripes help make hulls look lower and sleeker.

Also think about the sort of timber you might use. Opt either for mahogany or teak but never mix the two. And no matter which

11 Our smart, new-look forepeak. Once all the white surfaces had been painted, the previously prepared and varnished frames were bonded in with epoxy.

12 Our new, improved interior. As you can see, large, bright, white surfaces give a feeling of space and light. The inside of the hull has been insulated with carpet bonded to the hull with the usual carpet adhesive. It's inexpensive but extremely attractive.

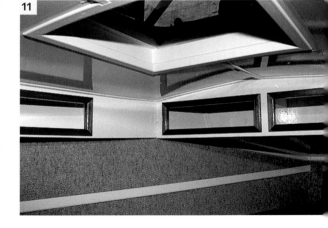

of the two you go for, combine them with contrasting, light surfaces or wood. Avoid grey or brown.

It's also best to try and avoid a cold, plasticky feel, both above and below decks. For example, if you have a fibreglass rubbing strake, you might add an aluminium strip on top, which can improve the appearance enormously.

Coloured hulls are quite popular at the moment and if you look at the paint manufacturers' brochures you'll find a huge range of shades to choose from. Some of the brochures also offer tips and hints about combining different colours and again, it does no harm to have a look at what they have to say.

TECHNICAL ASPECTS

Overhauling the outboard

In some cases, the outboard motor may be considerably older than the boat and for that reason have lots of things wrong with it, like streaks of rust, barnacles, leaking gaskets, and dirty or blocked filters. But the good news is that even a neglected engine can be brought back to life – as this chapter will show.

1 Spray lubricants creep below corrosion and moisture, making the engine easier to start.

An outboard can last for at least thirty years, and even a really tatty example can often be rejuvenated. It may need a thorough overhaul, but afterwards, should continue to give good service as long as you look after it.

2 If you can't check the engine in harbour, you can always run it in a large plastic bin instead. But be careful, and keep it in neutral! Check to see if the engine starts and runs smoothly, that no oil seeps from the shaft, whether water comes from the exhaust and listen for any unusual or unwanted noises.

3 The business-end of a spark plug tells you a lot about the condition of the engine. It should be light brown; if it isn't, there's something wrong. If possible, you should always check the plugs before buying a boat. But never grease the thread when screwing plugs back in; if you do the engine oil will burn itself into the grease.

4 Sooted plugs won't work properly because they allow electrical energy to escape from the surface of the electrode-isolators. You can easily remove the layer of soot with a steel brush. Gently force the bristles inside, then turn the plug a few times in each direction. Finally give the plug a good clean blast of air from a compressor.

5 After mechanical cleaning, wash the plug in petrol. You can also use thinners or paraffin. Dry the plug and again clean with compressed air. Check the gap of the electrode before putting the plug back into the engine, it should probably be around 0.6 or 0.7 millimetres but always refer to the manual.

A typical two-stroke engine is simple and easy to work on. Four-strokes and diesels, however, are better left in the hands of professional mechanics. With a two-stroke, all you need to do is look at the ignition, the carburettor and the propeller. So let's begin with the spark plugs. Once you've removed them, they can tell you if the engine is still basically OK. You want to see light brown deposits on the electrodes. If, instead, they look dark grey and oily, the engine has probably never been run at its normal operating temperature but has only been used for short trips while it was still cold. That's not healthy for the plugs or the combustion. So, once you've serviced it, remember, if you want to keep it in good condition, use it regularly, and for longer trips too. If you tend to use the engine only for manoeuvring in and out of harbours, you could switch to spark plugs with a higher calorific value. But plugs can also get oily if one of the leads is defective or if the compression is low. So first change the leads and if that doesn't solve the problem, have the compression checked. Heavily sooted spark plugs should always be exchanged for new ones in the course of a refit. It's possible to clean them, but that's only a temporary measure; something you might do if you were afloat, say, and ran into problems and forgot to bring spares.

Now for the carburettor. It's fairly complicated, but all you really need to know is where to find the main jet and fuel-filter. Both often get blocked. A test-run of the engine will also reveal if the revs at tick-over in neutral are right. Around 600 revs per minute is about the norm – but you might have to adjust it.

Finally, check the propeller and gears. Remove the propeller and check the mechanical parts for corrosion. Then take a close look at the gearbox. Are there any metal deposits in the oil? Is the shaft seal still intact? The following pictures show what you need to do.

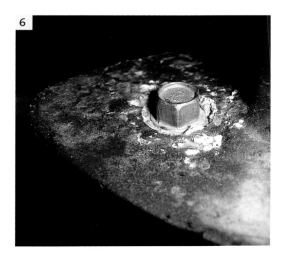

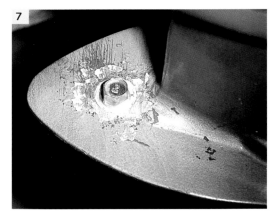

6 The leg, and particularly the anti-cavitation plate, are fairly vulnerable because two different metals – light alloy and stainless steel – live side by side here. And when saltwater enters the scenario, the resulting cocktail encourages corrosion beneath the paint. This process is enhanced if the leg is left in the water all the time.

7 The first step is to remove all the loose particles of paint and corrosion with a scraper, and finish off with sand or glass paper. I suggest you use a low-pressure aluminium-oxide spray. Don't worry too much about rough scratches and dents; they can simply be filled and sanded later on.

8 Having got right back to a good, sound base, you should first de-grease the surface thoroughly, then apply two or three coats of a good quality epoxy-based primer.

9 Once the epoxy primer has completely cured, you can freshen everything up with some aerosol paint from a spray can. You can either buy it from the engine manufacturer or in a car accessory shop. If you treat it to three or four coats – it should look like new. But for safety's sake, always remember to wear a mask.

10 Salt water can cause terrible havoc with any outboard so, when you're not using your engine, lift it completely clear of the water. This particular propeller attachment shows the sort of thing that happens if you leave it immersed for a period of time: the inevitable result is corrosion, marine growth, and barnacles.

11 Most propellers are usually mounted with self-locking nuts or nuts secured with a split pin. The engine shown here has a self-locking nut which you have to remove with a long box spanner. (The screwdriver adds leverage.) You should always replace it with a new nut afterwards.

12 As you can see here, the inner gasket is also damaged. Electrolysis has caused corrosion. However, in spite of that, you won't actually have to replace the propeller at this stage. It's reassuring to know that these sort of problems can be repaired without too much trouble.

13 The paint system you use on the metal is vitally important. Special epoxy-based primers like this are available which guarantee a long life. Always mix the paint and hardener in the recommended ratios, but only make up small amounts at a time, and remember to stay within the pot-life printed in the manufacturer's instructions.

14 A rotating steel brush in your power drill will quickly and easily remove any loose particles of paint and corrosion. Then, you simply de-grease the surface and apply three coats of primer with a soft brush. If you wanted to speed up the curing time, you could always use a hot air blower to heat up the air up to 60 degrees Celsius.

15 The hub itself has been attacked by corrosion. Again, you should clean it with the rotating steel brush but be particularly careful not to damage either the propeller shaft itself or the gasket which should be carefully examined at this stage. Naturally, there should be no oil leaks.

16 Two dissimilar metals in saltwater can often cause problems. This shaft is made of stainless steel, the propeller from alloy. As a preventative measure, you should cover the shaft liberally with waterproof grease, which not only lubricates but acts as a protective barrier. You should also turn the prop back and forth on the shaft a few times.

17 You should always paint the propeller before you put it back on. Again, the easiest option is to use an aerosol spray. Four coats should be enough. If the propeller remains in the water for longer periods, perhaps because the outboard lives on board in a well or trunk, paint it with antifouling.

18 The mechanism for tilting the engine can only work smoothly if you keep it properly and regularly greased. The best way to do this is to use a proper grease gun which forces lubricating grease into all the greasing points until the grease itself is squeezed sideways out of the bearings. Afterwards, remember to remove any excess with a cloth.

19 Clean the petrol-filter. First, remove the cover, then take out the fine filter and wash it in petrol. If you find any traces of resin-like remains in the filter, exchange it for a new one. For older engines, it might be a good idea to fit an extra filter somewhere in the fuel line.

20 Different metals need the right sacrificial anodes to prevent a reaction in salt water. You should always replace used anodes and never simply paint over them. It's also important to check on the state of the anode from time to time. If it doesn't degrade at all, it may be the wrong type – which means that electrolysis is probably attacking other parts of the engine.

21 Changing the oil. Check the old oil for metallic particles. If you don't find any, simply pour the new oil into the engine until it runs out of the overflow. After that, you then tighten both screws, having previously fitted them with new washers.

22 Engine brackets have really hard lives on small boats and are exposed to mechanical stress as well as attacks from salt and moisture – both of which can have a seriously detrimental effect particularly on the state of the varnish. That's why it pays to keep an eye on them and carry out regular maintenance.

23 For reasons of cost, no doubt, some manufacturers still use ordinary domestic-type bolts on engine brackets which inevitably start to rust, probably after one or two years. Bearing that in mind, it's really a false economy. You should always remove them, throw them away, and replace them with proper stainless steel alternatives.

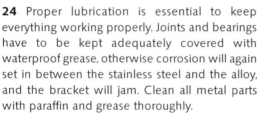

24 Proper lubrication is essential to keep everything working properly. Joints and bearings have to be kept adequately covered with waterproof grease, otherwise corrosion will again set in between the stainless steel and the alloy, and the bracket will jam. Clean all metal parts with paraffin and grease thoroughly.

25 The surface of this wooden bracket had been damaged but the core was still sound. Use a plane to smooth the surface, then sand and varnish six times. Instead of polyurethane varnish you could try a less brittle, more porous and flexible, oil-based product which might penetrate deeper and be less likely to flake off.

Repairing a teak deck

This chapter deals with some of the typical sort of problems you get with teak laid decks and how best to repair them. Remember, even small defects can have serious consequences. The earlier you deal with them, the less work will be involved.

The teak laid deck's deadliest enemy is water. As soon as it starts getting in under the wood on a permanent basis, rot will develop from

1 Look closely for signs of trouble. As you can see, this cleat is inadequately sealed underneath the base. That's why the wood stays wet.

underneath, and the timber will quickly degrade. During the winter months, water trapped in these trouble spots can also freeze, and get forced upwards as it expands, causing splits. Even weather resistant teak, which has a high oil content is unable to resist such a process for very long.

2 If a deck is cleaned only rarely in wet climates, it invariably goes green in places. Assuming the deck is sufficiently thick, and still has enough substance to it, the only proper remedy is sanding. However, a word of warning: you should never clean the teak deck with a high pressure cleaner. That only removes soft fibres from the wood, allowing fresh water to accumulate, and simply makes the problem worse.

These long-term problems can only be avoided by care and attention when laying the teak itself or by immediately repairing damaged areas when they come to light. Improperly sealed deck fittings like cleats or stanchions also often cause severe problems.

3a + 3b This strip has been secured with ordinary screws. The result is rust – as you can see in the left hand picture. When the plug falls out, the entire deck will have to be repaired.

That's why it's so important to always keep an eye open and, in particular, to look out for leaks or other tell-tale signs. As a case in point, experienced owners can often identify potential trouble spots by conducting an examination after a wet and windy passage or a rainy squall. Healthy wood will dry out far more quickly than damp or damaged areas.

The next step is to track down the source. If the problem has only been caused by a badly fixed deck fitting, the remedy is usually

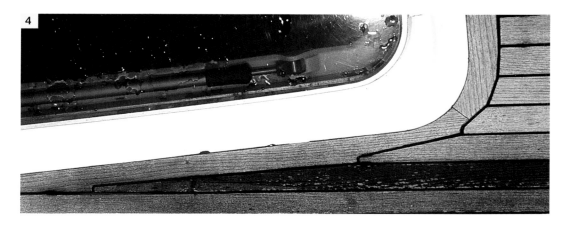

4 Danger signals. One badly sealed strip can endanger large areas. Water which gets in underneath the wood will also run under the neighbouring strips. A timely repair is essential.

5 If any part of the teak deck has been designed in such a way that it encourages puddles of water, the once pristine timber will quickly start to decay. This is a fundamental fault.

fairly straightforward. The fitting will have to be removed and put back in place then bedded down with adequate sealant. Using masking tape to cover the adjoining teak, you should apply the sealant and then position the fitting in place. At this stage you should only lightly tighten the screws leaving just a thin film of sealant between the deck and the fitting itself. The screws should only be tightened right up once the sealant has properly cured. Afterwards, any excess sealant around the edges of the fitting can easily be removed with a sharp knife.

Other potential problem areas are deck hatches, especially when the frame of the hatch has been screwed directly to the teak. A repair here can be carried out, in much the same way – and as previously outlined – and would be the same for any deck fitting.

Again, stanchions whose bases have been simply screwed directly to the teak are always potential trouble makers. The forces at work

6 If the teak is laid on plywood, the latter will begin to show through after a while. In this example, the timber cladding on this locker will have to be completely renewed.

7 The new covering can be made of pre-fabricated teak components with a chunky wooden framework.

8 If the seams are higher than the surrounding wood, they need to be cut back. Otherwise the sealant won't bond with the wood any more, allowing water to seep in underneath the wood.

here can be fairly considerable, partly because of the nature of the fitting and partly because of the leverage involved. For that reason, the bases of the stanchions should always be bolted directly to the deck rather than merely screwed to the teak. In practice, it's also better to lay the teak around the stanchions. To cope with the forces involved here, simply screwing into timber is wholly inadequate. A small plate of extremely hard rubber, about 4 millimetres thick, beneath the base of the stanchion can also help to distribute the forces, as well as seal it off from the adjoining timber. You may well have to deal with even bigger problems if – as already intimated – you discover that one or more strips of teak remain wet after a shower, after all the other areas have dried out. If you're lucky, the cause might simply be a leaky seam next to the strip in question. This is something that can easily be repaired, but it certainly pays to investigate the problem thoroughly, even if it means removing the strip completely.

If it looks sound and is still hard under-neath, then it can be safely re-laid after the deck has been primed and subsequently covered in sealant. The first job is to rub down the underside of the strip to remove any old bits of sealant. Lay it down in its bed of fresh sealant, and also seal off the seams on both sides, then finally sand the wood down. If the strip is beginning to degrade or is already rotten, then this particular strip – or maybe even the entire section of the deck – will have to be renewed.

An alternative method, rather than

bedding the strip down in sealant, is to use thickened epoxy resin. The only problem here is that it's not in the slightest bit flexible so the chances are that small cracks will develop in the wood over a period of time.

To carry out repairs like this, the old wooden plugs as well as the screws underneath will have to be removed. But how on earth do you get them out? You can't simply lever them out with a screwdriver, because that would damage the edges of the holes which, in turn, would make it impossible for the new plugs to fit properly or form a decent seal. The preferred option is to drill a five millimetre hole through the centre of the plug right down to the screw underneath, then insert a six millimetre screw. With luck, the plug will then lift itself out of the hole on its own.

If things don't go according to plan however, the whole operation becomes a little more complicated. Perhaps the plug was glued in with epoxy resin? If so, all you can do is to completely drill it out. Use a wood drill with a bit approximately 2 millimetres larger than the original plug.

Sadly, there were times when a number of yards fitted teak decks with mild steel screws or iron fastenings that began to rust as soon as the wooden plugs on top began to wear. Teak quickly stains when rust seeps up through the thin wood to the surface above. In the next stage of the process, the thin plugs will probably fall off altogether.

If your deck shows tell-tale signs of screws rusting away underneath the teak, the best remedy is to replace them. Having said that, it's only possible to remove the old screws if the corrosion is limited. If the screws are already so rusty that the heads fall off or you can't turn them with the screwdriver, all that remains is to drill them all out. This in turn will leave large holes in the fibreglass deck.

If it's possible to remove all the old screws without any problems, two options remain. As

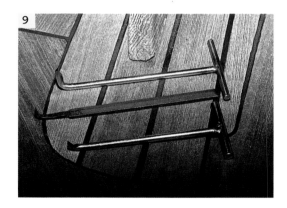

9 If the seams do need to be re-sealed, you'll need to rake out the old sealant. To do that, the simplest and cheapest way is to use tools which can be made at home.

10 To find out exactly how much the teak has worn away, you can always measure it like this.

long as the teak is still sound and sufficiently thick, simply drill the new holes slightly deeper and re-lay the old teak decking, using new stainless steel screws to fasten it. They should also be bedded in sealant, as indeed should the teak itself. If the teak however has already worn thin, the only option left is to completely renew the deck. If that's the situation you find yourself in, it's worth considering a pre-fabricated teak deck because there's a range to choose from and because it's a slightly more economical solution.

Another potential problem is the sealant itself. Ideally, as the name implies, it should seal the seams and stay extremely flexible but still bond well with the wood. The problems begin when the teak begins to wear. Sealant will now protrude above the teak strips and be exposed to sideways pressure. At some point, its bond with the wood will break down and the deck will start to leak.

To stop that happening, you must remove any excess sealant using a very sharp knife or a small plane until the sealant itself is flush with the wood once more. Unfortunately, you can't sand the sealant because that would only make the surface porous.

The method mentioned above is only practical when the seams are still watertight. If the sealant has already lost its bond with the wood, it will have to be completely renewed. A special tool shaped like a hook is used to rake out the old sealant. If you have to remove a great deal, it might be easier to use a small circular saw using a batten as a guide.

There are two basic ways of filling the seams. One is to use sealant from a tin, covering the entire deck and then, once it's cured, sanding it down. The other is to cover the strips of wood with masking tape and to fill the seams with a hand pressure gun. In the first case, the time consuming and really laborious bit is the sanding at the end. In the second case, the problem is masking all the strips of wood before you start.

The wood can be worn off more in some places than in others, maybe because of different wear patterns or because someone cleaned the decks the wrong way – using high pressure hoses perhaps, or scrubbing along the grain instead of across. As long as the rest of the deck is still in good condition, sanding can still even out indentations up to 3 millimetres deep. The main concern at this stage is the condition of the plugs and screws. Hopefully, all will be well, otherwise they might have to be replaced. It's wise to remove all the deck fittings before sanding. That's the only way to ensure that all the strips of teak are flush with one another. Not only that, an uncluttered deck is so much easier to work on.

If you find degraded teak sitting on a plywood substructure, it's not worth trying to repair it. Until a few years ago, some yards tried to make budget-priced boats look more sophisticated – and the best way to do that, they thought, was with sprinklings of 'cheap' unsophisticated teak on ply. Locker lids, cockpit floors and other areas were covered with the stuff – but what seemed perfectly acceptable in the first few years, soon lost its appeal and, in the end, turned out to be a false economy. The very thin layer of teak they used wore away extremely quickly revealing the cheap plywood underneath. All too often, the plywood began to rot beneath the much more resistant teak.

Low budget components like these are usually beyond repair. The best remedy is a new teak layer made of strips that should be at least 6 millimetres thick. Take special care with the end strips and the timber frames on lids and lockers since they take the most punishment. Investing in good quality timber and materials will pay off in the long run.

When thinking about buying a second hand boat with teak laid decks or, indeed, other teak components, you should inspect them extremely carefully. To that end, it's always a good idea to carry out a few simple tests. Pouring water over the teak deck, for instance, is absolutely essential, if you want to assess its condition and uncover any potential problems. And there's no need to feel in the least inhibited about it; after all, repairing teak decks is both expensive and highly labour intensive, so it's perfectly reasonable to take a good, close-up look at the deck of any boat you might eventually buy.

Laying teak decks

Modern methods have made it much easier to lay a teak deck, but, of course, you can still do it the traditional way if you prefer.

1 Choosing carefully. Selecting the right timber is all important. Only a fifth of the trunk will be good enough to use for the deck.

To make a professional job of fitting a teak deck was a real challenge for every boat-builder until not so very long ago. Hundreds of teak strips or planks had to be sawn, bent, fitted with thousands of screws and then glued. Every single screw had to be closed off with a wooden plug. And every single plug had to be faired by hand. Then, after that, there was still hundreds of metres of caulking to be completed; the deck also had to be cleaned and sanded. This meant a lot of manual work, which, of course, cost a great deal of money – so it's little wonder that teak decks are regarded as a luxury by many sailors even today.

However, the industry is changing fast. Granted, many small, individual boat yards that only produce a limited number of yachts still lay their teak decks in the time-honoured, traditional way. But, having changed their building methods accordingly, plenty of the bigger yards now make full use of the opportunities offered by industrialised mass-production. Many famous builders, including firms like Hallberg-Rassy or Nautor only use pre-fabricated teak decks which are glued to the boats under pressure from a vacuum.

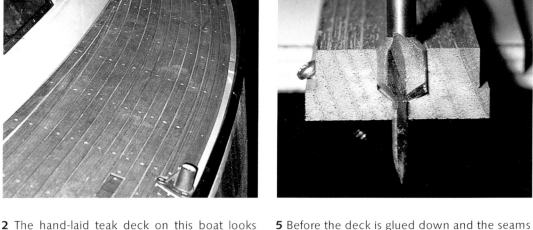

2 The hand-laid teak deck on this boat looks perfect. Each strip has been cut and fitted individually.

3 The deck beams are first covered in plywood, and then the teak deck laid on top.

4 The annular rings should run vertically through the timber. If they don't, the strips won't be suitable for laid decking.

5 Before the deck is glued down and the seams filled in, all teak strips are cut to size and laid out on the deck. Check the run of the seams.

6 This special drill allows you to cut the hole for the screw and the wider hole for the head in one go.

If done properly, both methods will yield satisfying results. Assuming the wood has been chosen carefully and is thick enough, pre-fabricated decks are every bit as durable as their classic cousins and can last for 20 years or more. That's largely because the relevant vacuum bonding technology – which is in use all over the world – is now generally accepted as an international industry standard, so, these days, critical generalisations about the technology, which previously, might have had more than a grain of truth in

them, are simply misplaced.

However, as I say, that only applies to today's standards in boat building. As already intimated, five or ten years ago, things were very different, and a lot of decks were less than professional. Reports were even published in the marine press about boat yards which were using screws made from normal mild steel to save costs, hoping they might not succumb to rust their smart, wooden plugs. Their trust was misplaced. Years later, of course, the problems begin to

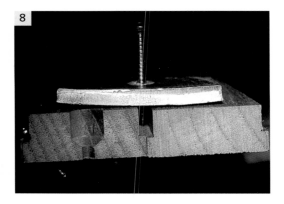

7 When all strips fit correctly, the deck is covered in glue and the numbered strips are then screwed down. The deck should be finished in one day.

8 A covering board is used to press the teak strips onto the deck until the glue has cured. The covering board can be fixed with weights or cheap screws that are later removed.

emerge. Rusting screws expand. They force the plugs from their sockets and have to be replaced, more often than not by first drilling them out. In the worst case, the entire deck will have to be renewed.

Similarly, there were a few technical problems when the new kind of industrial bonding techniques were first introduced. Some manufacturers experimented with cheap backing materials such as plywood – and the vacuum bonding technique itself had yet to be perfected. That caused more problems. Some areas of the deck could be less well bonded than others, for example, which meant that moisture would creep in under the wood and the structure would start to rot from the bottom up. This was yet another disastrous weakness which, as with the sub-standard screws, could necessitate the renovation or replacement of the entire deck.

Yet another common mistake was the use of the wrong sealant in the seams, but at least this was a little less serious, and easy to spot in time. If the consistency of the sealant was inappropriate, the wood could wear away more quickly, leaving the seams sticking up proud between the timber strips. That made them incredibly vulnerable, so they started to break up, which in turn, left gaps for water to penetrate underneath the wood.

Cases such as these have led to a certain and understandable unease amongst buyers and owners alike. Precisely how many boats might be affected is difficult to say at this stage; it could be hundreds or only a handful. But each individual case that crops up in conversation, whether in yacht club or marina bar, will inevitably trigger yet another discussion and fuel further speculation. Incidentally, replacing an existing but damaged teak deck is always more expensive than fitting a new one to a fibreglass boat.

But how can you judge the quality of a teak deck, and how can you avoid expensive repairs later?

There are many different kinds of teak deck on the market today, both the timber as well as the construction technique may vary. The range of options begins with cheap decks – made from straight, teak strips that end up looking square and unsophisticated – to superbly crafted creations with curved, flowing strips of teak, neat butts, and a smart central section along the centreline. With the

9 In this case, the strips have been directly screwed into the sealant. The screws remain in the deck and are later covered with wooden plugs.

10 The plugs should not be removed from the strip before they are inserted. To fit them, press them into the hole vertically, tap them and then hammer home.

11 Use a sharp chisel to cut the plug off carefully, layer by layer. Any remaining bit can be faired in with sandpaper.

12 The deck can only be sanded once the sealant has cured completely. Finally, the deck fittings are replaced.

traditional method, all the teak strips are individually sawn and fastened to the deck. They vary in width between 35 and 40 millimetres. The more they bend, the narrower they should be. On an old IOR type boat with a big 'belly', 35 millimetre strips are the norm. The long deck of a narrower modern IMS boat, on the other hand, would be perfectly happy with 40 millimetre strips.

The thickness of the teak, on, say, a 10-metre sailing yacht, should be around 10 millimetres on deck and 8 millimetres on the coachroof. Remember: when the finished deck has been sanded, about one to two millimetres of timber will be removed. Only then will the strips be completely flush with each other. Obviously, the thicker the deck is to start with, the more often you can sand it.

13

13 This is a cross-section through a pre-fabricated deck. The strips are held together by a thin carrier foil which can also be made of teak.

14 A teak deck being glued on under vacuum pressure using an industrial production method.

Expensive yards and larger yachts will therefore often have decks with teak 12 to 14 millimetres thick.

Even more important than the actual thickness of the wood is the position and intensity of the annular rings in the planks or strips. They should be as near as possible perpendicular to the ends so they can expand horizontally when the wood moves. Unless the strips are cut like this, the wood can warp and twist when wet. This basic and extremely important principle is sometimes ignored on production boats. However, it's easy to spot wood which has been cut in the wrong way. As long as the grain runs parallel to the seams, and over the entire length of the strip, the job has been done correctly. If the grain runs out of the strip or changes along the way, you should be wary and proceed with caution.

Round, shell-like annular rings on the surface of the strips or even knotholes are sure signs of a cheap, unprofessionally laid deck. Decks like these will wear most unevenly and with their soft surfaces facing upwards, will be easily damaged. If you follow traditional methods, the strips are bent on deck, pressed in place, drilled and screwed down one after the other. After this initial, 'dry' run, the strips are numbered and removed again. The sealant is then applied generously over the entire deck; finally, the strips are primed underneath and screwed back in place. In this way, everything gets thickly covered in sealant. The screw heads are then covered in teak plugs (glued in with epoxy). The plugs are faired down and the seams filled with the appropriate sealant. Once the sealant has cured completely – between two and eight days depending on manufacturer and type – the deck can be sanded.

Only then can you start fitting the deck hardware. A pre-fabricated teak deck is easier, quicker and cheaper to fit, both when building a new yacht and when refitting one later.

Today, you'll find a number of large, good quality pre-fabricated teak decks are on the market. The strips are held together with a thin foil or merely by the sealant between the seams. Decks like these come in large boards about 6 millimetres thick, and can be bonded

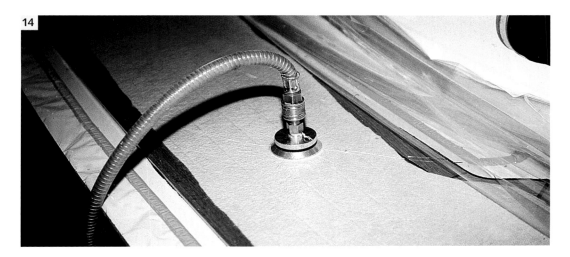

straight onto the existing deck, using a vacuum or lead weights. Since this does away with screw heads, you can use the full thickness of the teak which can be sanded several times.

You might see a few plugs in decks like these, but they only cover the screws that held the deck in place temporarily and usually, would be subsequently removed. The holes they leave behind are filled with epoxy and plugged, which means that a bonded deck can look just like a traditionally screwed one, but without the danger of screws eventually becoming exposed through abrasion and wear.

Apart from entire decks, you can also use teak boards like this for hatch covers, cockpit lockers and coamings, as well as cockpit floors and the like. To cover small areas in pre-fabricated teak decks, you can cut cardboard templates and then have the decking pieces made to the right size. It's important to remove all the deck fittings from the area concerned. This may cost you a bit of time but save you money later on. Some manufacturers of pre-fabricated teak decks also store the deck layouts of some of the more popular production yachts in their computers.

With pre-fabricated teak components, there are two basic methods you can use to fit them to the deck. The cheaper option is to leave a small gap between teak and cabin sides, where the teak strips end straight without butts. The other option is slightly more expensive and involves the use of butt ends and finishing tight against the cabin sides; this method looks exactly like a traditionally laid teak deck and it's hard to tell the difference.

But even despite pre-fabrication, these decks are far from cheap. You'll easily reach a four-digit figure if you want to fit a new teak deck to a 30-foot yacht. Having said that, a traditionally hand-laid teak deck will be about a third more expensive. These prices also reflect the huge number of off-cuts incurred in the production process. Only about 20 percent of any teak trunk is really suitable for a decent deck. On top of that, reputable manufacturers will choose their wood carefully to maintain high quality.

Not surprisingly perhaps, because of the high prices, many boat-builders and manufacturers are looking for alternative types of wood. Some are using iroko and kambala, but these are harder to work with than teak and don't look quite as good. So, for the time being, the majority of laid decks will still be made of teak.

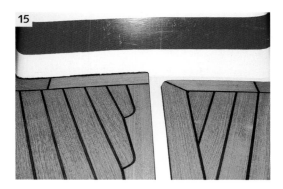

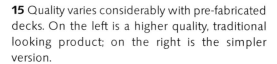

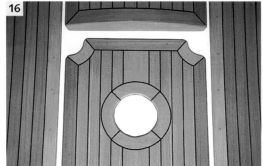

15 Quality varies considerably with pre-fabricated decks. On the left is a higher quality, traditional looking product; on the right is the simpler version.

16 All shapes and sizes are possible in teak. This is a cockpit floor with a steering pedestal.

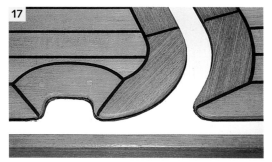

17 Looking good: many manufacturers offer custom made strips that are individually fabricated to size. Take great care when measuring these strips to ensure a perfect fit later on.

What makes teak so special and where does it come from

Origin: Teak trees grow in South-East Asia (Burma, Thailand, India). They grow up to 40 metres high, in which case they deliver 20 metre long, clean trunks. Their diameter is then between 0.5 and one metre.

Wood-types: The wood types are named after their origin (Burma-Teak, Java-Teak and so on) as well as after the way they grew – there are natural teak trees as well as teak plantations. They can be identified by the distance of their yearly rings. These are about six to seven millimetres apart in the case of plantation teak that is cut after 30 to 40 years. In natural teak that grew to be 70 to 80 years old, the rings are only two to four millimetres apart.

Description: The core wood is yellowish, the rest light to dark brown. This colour disappears after a while and is replaced by a silvery-greyish tint.

Characteristics: Teak is perfect for building boats and ships as it does not shrink nearly as much as all other boat-building timbers. It is very much weather-proof, dries quickly, is not slippery even when wet and insulates well against cold and noise.

Cost: Teak is easily the world's most important high class timber and is in great demand. The price is accordingly high. One cubic metre of cut teak will cost anything from £1400 ($2350) upwards, this is twice as much as the price of Mahogany. And only 20 per cent of each trunk can be used for teak decks – this makes it even more expensive.

CE-Rules and Regulations for part-built and home-built boats

This brief synopsis has been taken from the 'Regulations of the European Parliament for Leisure Boats' – (94/25/EG, spring 2001). Amateur boat builders should pay particular attention to the paragraph about 'special issues' which highlights two basic categories.

1. Part-built boats for home completion

The first important point to remember is that no boat in a part-built state will be granted CE certification.

Having said that, a professional yard may build a hull and deliver it, along with a building certificate, to a customer who may then choose to complete it and subsequently use the boat himself. But if that's indeed what he decides to do, the customer then has to make a choice. He can either ignore the fact that the boat was, in essence, professionally built by a yard, and simply treat it as a wholly amateur-project, for which the relevant rules of this particular section apply.

Alternatively, he can act like a boatyard, in which case he will have to comply with all relevant tests and regulations. The advantages of the second alternative are two-fold: he can always sell the boat later on, and, of course, if he does so, since the boat has a proper CE certificate, it should command a higher price.

Self-built boats

These constitute a special case in the Regulations, and don't have to be tested and certified in the way that professionally built boats do. The downside is that, after completion, boats like these can't be sold within the first five years. The reason for the ruling is to avoid the possibility of a grey market. However, whether this particular rule is legal or not remains to be seen. As it is, there's a question mark over it because it restricts the use of a person's property. Similarly, there could be special circumstances, which might make compliance difficult or undesirable. It's possible to imagine a number of unforseen situations, such as death or illness etc which might force someone to sell a particular boat at a particular time.

By the same token, the question as to whether a private, amateur builder can actually build a boat and fulfil all the CE norms which apply to professionally-built product, is one that remains unanswered. As it stands, the European Commission fails to differentiate between amateur and professional builders. Either way, the international consensus seems to make the assumption that any amateur builder can indeed act like a professional yard. He must however find an official body that will test and certify his product. But any such agency will take into consideration the size of the boat and its intended use – and some of these authorities may apply criteria that amateurs will find simply impossible to comply with.

Whatever the definitive interpretation, everyone, including amateur boat builders, should always take all the relevant rules and regulations into consideration.

Index